Networking and Data Communications Laboratory Manual

Frances S. Grodzinsky, *Editor*

An Alan R. Apt Book

Prentice Hall
Upper Saddle River, New Jersey 07458

Library of Congress Cataloging-in-Publication Data

Grodzinsky, Frances Schlamowitz
    Networking and data communications laboratory manual / by
Frances S. Grodzinsky.
       p. cm.
    Includes bibliographical references and index.
    ISBN 0-13-011702-1
    1. Data transmission systems—Handbooks, manuals, etc
2. Computer networks—Handbooks, manuals, etc.   I. Title
TK5105 .G757   1999
004.6'078—ddc21   98-458999
                                CIP

Publisher: *Alan Apt*
Editor: *Laura Steele*
Production editor: *Edward DeFelippis*
Editor-in-chief: *Marcia Horton*
Managing editor: *Eileen Clark*
Assistant vice president of production and manufacturing: *David W. Riccardi*
Art director: *Jayne Conte*
Cover designer: *Bruce Kenselaar*
Manufacturing buyer: *Pat Brown*

©1999 by Prentice-Hall, Inc.
Upper Saddle River, New Jersey 07458

The author and publisher of this book have used their best efforts in preparing this book. These efforts include the development, research, and testing of the theories and programs to determine their effectiveness. The author and publisher make no warranty of any kind, expressed or implied, with regard to these programs or the documentation contained in this book. The author and publisher shall not be liable in any event for incidental or consequential damages in connection with, or arising out of, the furnishing, performance, or use of these programs.

Printed in the United States of America

10 9 8 7 6 5 4 3

ISBN 0-13-011702-1

PRENTICE-HALL INTERNATIONAL (UK) LIMITED, *LONDON*
PRENTICE-HALL OF AUSTRALIA PTY. LIMITED, *SYDNEY*
PRENTICE-HALL CANADA INC., *TORONTO*
PRENTICE-HALL HISPANOAMERICANA, S.A., *MEXICO*
PRENTICE-HALL OF INDIA PRIVATE LIMITED, *NEW DELHI*
PRENTICE-HALL OF JAPAN, INC., *TOKYO*
PEARSON EDUCATION ASIA PTE. LTD., *SINGAPORE*
EDITORA PRENTICE-HALL DO BRASIL, LTDA., *RIO DE JANEIRO*

INTRODUCTION

We are pleased to present several laboratory exercises for a range of courses in computer networks and data communications. The need for such a book grew out of discussions with faculty participating in a two-week National Science Foundation–sponsored computer network workshop, held at Michigan State University during the summers of 1994 and 1996. From these discussions, it became clear that faculty involved in teaching undergraduate networking and data communications courses wanted a laboratory component. It was also recognized that appropriate computer network exercises were not readily available in traditional textbooks. The workshop participants chose to pool their efforts by assembling a collection of lab assignments previously used in their individual courses. Since these participants came from a wide range of institutions (small colleges to large universities), a very diverse set of lab assignments was presented for consideration.

Many of these assignments are designed to enhance the understanding of concepts/principles discussed in texts, whereas others may serve to emphasize network experiments in the areas of network performance, simulations, and other topics that may not be directly covered. This variety of network laboratories will enable potential users to select exercises from several levels of sophistication. We also include a sufficient amount of documentation for each lab, along with instructions. Each lab assignment is presented in a common format that includes the setup, along with hardware and software requirements.

The lab assignments presented in this manual are quite varied and reflect the different emphases and texts chosen by the workshop participants for their courses. Over 15 of the 20 participants have contributed to this endeavor. The labs can be effectively used with any networking or data communication textbook to reinforce fundamental concepts and theories associated with the network physical layer, data link layer, network layer, transport layer, and application layer. Additionally, some labs are devoted to Comnet III simulations, Internet activities, NOVELL NetWare, and PC hardware. Over 40 different labs are presented, some of which can be used to emphasize data communications, while others may be more suitable to networking. These labs are also different in regard to the amount of programming required. This affords valuable network experience for students both with and without programming skills.

Because networking is changing so rapidly, it is our intention to revise this lab manual in the future according to the feedback received from the networking community. Furthermore, we invite others to submit interesting labs to the editor, so that a richer set of networking exercises can be made available to the undergraduate networking faculty across the country and abroad.

Herman D. Hughes, Ph.D.
Professor of Computer Science
Michigan State University

CONTENTS

PREFACE

This laboratory manual is a work of dedication and collaboration by faculty from universities and colleges across the country who teach networking and data communications. We met at Michigan State University in 1994 and have been working for the last four years to create a practical component that can be used in a variety of networking and data communication courses with a variety of texts. Each lab indicates the audience and duration as well as the equipment needed. We have tried to make these exercises as flexible as possible and have added suggestions for modifications that can either increase or decrease the level of difficulty of the lab.

Many people made this book possible. I would like to thank Laura Steele and Sandy Hackenson at Prentice Hall for facilitating the publication of this book. I would also like to thank my colleagues who developed and tested these labs in their courses, who modified, edited, and revised them and then came up with new labs to accommodate the changes in technology that have occurred in these four years. We all would like to thank our networking and data communications students who helped us by testing and debugging these labs.

I would like to personally thank my present and former students Christopher Beyer, Darshan Toolsidass, Daniel Arnold, Brian Banet, Sherman Corning, Bonnie Schulte and James Barlow who added to the ideas for my labs, tested them, created and ran the sunflower student Web site, and were just there to help out.

We hope that these labs provide your students with as much insight into the theory and practice of networking and data communication as they have ours. There is a contributing authors list with e-mail addresses at the end of the book. Feel free to contact the individual authors if you have any questions about the labs. For labs that need supplementary files, go to the prenhall.com Web site and search for the book.

Frances S. Grodzinsky
Professor of Computer Science and Information Technology
Sacred Heart University
Fairfield, CT
grodzinskyf@sacredheart.edu

PART I

PHYSICAL LAYER

1.1 Bandwidth

by

William Teter

Objective: To understand how bandwidth of an analog signal affects the amount of detectable digitized data that can be encoded into the analog signal using Fourier series.

Brief Description: Two exercises that use Maple V software to examine analog and digital signals.

Audience: Students should know calculus. The Maple interface is variable among platforms. A Maple novice may require a lab aide familiar with Maple to untangle confusion.

Equipment: Many computer platforms support Maple. The lab uses the plot command extensively, so a monitor capable of graphics is essential.

Software: This lab is intended to be done in Maple V release 3 using a set of procedures and constants defined in a file called bw.m. To begin the lab you should read this file into the Maple workspace with a command like: read `a:bw.m`. Note the back quote! The file bw.txt contains a text version of the procedures and variables that are defined on bw.m.

Duration: One and a half hours.

PROCEDURE:

MATHEMATICAL BACKGROUND:

Any periodic continuous function can be approximated by adding together constant multiples of the sinusoidal functions. The function obtained is called a linear combination of the particular functions that are added.

The basic *sinusoidal functions* are

$$s_n(t) = \frac{1}{\sqrt{p}}\sin(n\,t) \text{ and } s_{-n}(t) = \frac{1}{\sqrt{p}}\cos(n\,t) \text{ where n is a positive}$$

integer and the *constant function* is $s_0(t) = \frac{1}{\sqrt{2p}}$.

EXERCISE 1:

Use Maple to graph several sinusoids s(i,t) where i will take on integer values and t is the real parameter between -Pi and Pi. The Maple function s(i,t) is the i'th sinusoid $s_i(t)$. The function s(i,t) is already defined. You may look at its definition with:

```
> op(s);
```

Plot several sinusoids:

```
> plot(s(2,t),t=-Pi..Pi);
> plot({s(-4,t), s(0,t),s(2,t)}, t=-Pi..Pi);
```

Pi is a predefined Maple constant. Maple is case sensitive, so pi is not the same as Pi (only the latter works).

Explain the effect of n on the basic sinusoids s(n,t).

_____

_____

_____

_____

_____

The frequency of a sinusoid is the number of times the graph repeats itself in the interval from -Pi to Pi. What is the frequency of:

s(3,t) _____

s(-1,t)_____

s(0,t) _____

MORE MATHEMATICS

Our next objective is to find a linear combination of the sinusoids s_is that best approximates a given digital signal. We will use 1 and –1 as our binary values, rather than 0 and 1. In your Maple workspace, define a digital datum as a list of 1s and –1s. (Always use dd as the name of this list, since it is a global variable used in procedures that derive other functions.)

```
>   dd:=[-1,1,1,1,-1,-1,1,1];
```

The length of the list is arbitrary. You can examine the associated digital signal ds(t) with the plot command:

```
>plot(ds(t),t=-Pi..Pi);
```

This digital signal is not very continuous, but it can still be approximated by linear combinations of the sinusoids s_is. Basically, the more sinusoids you use, the better the approximation. To find the constants involved in the linear combination of sinusoids, we use what is called the orthonormality property of the sinusoids. Use Maple to compute the integral of $s_i(t) * s_j(t)$ on the interval between -Pi and Pi. To compute

$$\int_{-Pi}^{Pi} s_3(t) * s_{-4}(t) \ dt$$

the Maple command is

```
>   evalf(int(s(3,t)*s(-4,t),t=-Pi..Pi));
```

What do you get for the integral of $s_i(t) * s_j(t)$ if $i = j$?_____

What do you get if i and j are different? _____

What if i or j is 0? _____

What if i and j are both 0?_____

Let ds(t) be a digitized signal as above. Let us find a linear combination of all the sinusoids with frequency less than or equal to n that best approximates ds(t). We are looking for the constants $\{c_i\}_{i=-n..n}$, called the Fourier coefficients, such that

$$ds(t) = \sum_{i=-n}^{n} c_i \, s_i(t)$$

If we multiply both sides by $s_j(t)$ and then integrate between -Pi and Pi, we find for each j that

$$\int_{-Pi}^{Pi} s_j(t) * ds(t) \ dt = \sum_{i=-n}^{n} \int_{-Pi}^{Pi} s_j(t) * c_i * s_i(t) \ dt$$

$$= \sum_{i=-n}^{n} c_i * \int_{-Pi}^{Pi} s_j(t) * s_i(t) \ dt = c_j$$

The procedure fc (fourier coefficients) computes these constants and stores them in an array which is passed as an actual parameter. The array c must be declared prior to using fc.

```
> c:=array(-50..50);
```

Both lf and hf are global constants used in the procedure fc that delimits the low frequency and high frequency, respectively, for the Fourier coefficients. Leave lf at 1:

```
> lf:=1;
```

and set hf to 50.

```
> hf:=50;
```

Compute the Fourier coefficients with

```
> fc(c);
```

The Fourier series function fs(t) is then automatically defined using the coefficients from the array c.

Graph both the digital signal ds(t) and its Fourier approximation fs(t) with

```
> plot({ds(t), fs(t)}, t=-Pi..Pi);
```

The array of coefficients is called the spectrum of the Fourier series. You can look at the spectrum with

```
>  plot(c[i], i= -hf ..hf);
```

EXERCISE 2:

Set dd to [-1,1,1,-1,1,1,1,-1] and find the minimum bandwidth (hf) so that the Fourier series fs(t) approximates ds(t) well enough so that the digital data can be recovered from fs(t). *Hint:* set hf to some number, compute fc(c), then plot ({ds(t), fs(t)}, t=-Pi..Pi). Repeat this exercise with the data dd:=[-1,1,-1,1,-1,1,-1,1]:

_____

_____

_____

_____

_____

To decide mathematically what data is encoded in the function fs(t), one could make a list of the average values of the function fs(t) over each of eight subintervals of the interval from -Pi to Pi. The average of a function is just the integral of the function over the subinterval divided by the length of the interval. In this case we are concerned only about the sign of the average, so we can use the Maple command:

```
> [seq(sign(int(fs(t),t=part(i-1)..part(i))),i=1..nops(dd))];
```

This Maple command has the unpleasant side effect of leaving $i = 9$. In the plot command

```
plot(c[i],i=-hf..hf);
```

i must be an unassigned variable. To unassign i, the command is

```
> i:= 'i';
```

Procedures and variables defined in bw.m include:

$s(i,t)$ — The i'th sinusoid function with parameter t. The sine functions use positive i, negative i's produce the cosines.

dd — List of binary data with values from $\{-1,1\}$.

c — An array used to hold Fourier coefficients.

hf — High-frequency limit for computing Fourier coefficients.

lf — Low-frequency limit for computing Fourier coefficients.

part — part (i) returns the x coordinate of the i'th point on the interval [-Pi, Pi] as i varies from 0 to nops(dd). nops(dd) is the length of the list dd.

fc — fc(c) computes the Fourier coefficients into the array c for the digital signal corresponding to the data in dd using hf and lf.

fs — The function fs(t) is a Fourier series using coefficients in array c summed from lf to hf.

ds — The function ds(t) is the digital signal associated with data in dd. The domain of ds is [-Pi, Pi].

mint — The function mint (i,a,b) returns the integral of s(i,t) for t in [a,b].

1.2 Simulation and Analysis of Pulse Code Modulation (PCM)

by

Peter Sanderson

Objective: This programming exercise will help you understand how Pulse Code Modulation (PCM) is used to transmit an analog signal over a digital medium, and the effects of alternative PCM encodings on the quality of the reconstructed analog signal.

Brief Description: This exercise will compare three different PCM methods for digital transmission of an analog data transmission signal. Your program will simulate the transmission of a character string from sender A to receiver B. The goal is to compare the analog signal sent by modem A with the analog signal received by modem B (ignoring noise), under three different PCM methods, all based on a 128-level scale: full 7-bit PCM, 4-bit differential PCM, and 1-bit delta modulation. These methods are described on pages 121–123 of Tanenbaum's *Computer Networks* (third edition).[1] The methods are compared by computing the average and standard deviation of the absolute difference between the transmitted (original) and received (reconstructed) analog signals. The difference is calculated at each PCM sampling point (125 microseconds). Time and all signals are simulated in software. This assignment requires a substantial design and programming effort and should be solved by teams of two students.

Audience: This laboratory exercise comes from the upper-division undergraduate elective course, Theory of Telecommunications. Its prerequisite is the Data Structures course. It is intended mainly for computer science majors having a strong mathematics and physics background. It is also recommended for computer information systems majors who have taken a networks course and desire a more in-depth study of networking fundamentals.

Equipment: None. This simulation exercise can be programmed using any available language. Its output can be imported to a spreadsheet for analysis and graphing.

Duration: Two weeks.

---

[1] Professors may use the description of PCM offered in other texts as well.

PROCEDURE:

This exercise will compare three different PCM (Pulse Code Modulation) methods for digital transmission of an analog data transmission signal. Your program will simulate the transmission of a character string from sender A to receiver B. You may program this individually or with a partner.

A's modem is given a bit sequence to transmit. For this exercise, ignore start bits, stop bits and parity. The signal goes out onto a voice-grade telephone cable according to these specifications: use an AC carrier of 600 Hz having an amplitude that ranges from -10 volts to +10 volts. Apply the signal to the carrier using an ASK (amplitude shift keying, amplitude modulation) scheme which multiplies the carrier amplitude by the bit value (see Fig. 2-18(b)). Transmit at 300 bps.

When the signal reaches the end office, it is digitized by a codec using PCM at a rate of 8000 samples per second. The signal is transmitted on a T1 carrier (this fact is used in your solution) to B's end office, where a second codec translates it back to an analog signal for transmission to B's modem.

The goal is to compare the analog signal sent by modem A with the analog signal received by modem B (ignoring noise), under three different PCM methods, all based on a 128-level scale: full 7-bit PCM, 4-bit differential PCM, and 1-bit delta modulation.

This will require some analysis on your part; the simulation is not very difficult but contains a lot of details. I suggest the program be controlled by a time variable which is updated upon each PCM sample. At this time, the transmitted analog signal value (in volts) can be calculated by a function, and the digital signal value calculated from that by another function. A third function will transform the digital signal value back to an analog value, which is then compared to the original. Use the language and compiler of your choice, indicating in the program's identifying comments what they are.

Lab Report should include:

1. The average and standard deviation of the absolute difference between the sent and received analog signal, as calculated at each PCM sampling point, for each of the three PCM methods. Your result should be based on transmission of the ASCII string (transmit eight bits per character) representing the famous first telephonic message: *Watson, come here, I want you.*

2. A plot, on a line or bar chart, using an interesting 40-sample (.005 seconds) interval of the original analog signal plus the reconstructed analog signal using each of the three PCM methods.

3. A paragraph summarizing your evaluation of the performance of the three PCM methods. If any appear to be seriously deficient, explain why.

4. All source and executable files.

1.3 Summary of the Next Seven Exercises

by

Shakil Akhtar

The next seven lab exercises offer implementations of LAN experiments in a low-cost networking environment. They may be used either as a group or independently. Although the network device used in the laboratory is a serial device interface on several Motorola 68000-based microcomputers (PT68K2 systems), serial devices on any PC system could be used. Experiments have been designed by using the common RS-232 interfaces. The set of experiments consists of CSMA/CD (Carrier Sense Multiple Access with Collision Detection) and Token Bus implementations of LAN protocols. The network speed is limited to 19.2 Kbps due to the limitations of the serial ports. However, as the main purpose in developing this laboratory is to teach students how the different communication protocols work, the speed of the network is of little significance.

The transmission media over which the protocol runs is the twisted-pair line, mainly because of the simplicity of installation and maintenance. Since the speed of the network is significantly lower than the limitations of the twisted pair, very little signal disruption is expected. The transmit and receive lines are connected together to provide for a bidirectional link to the network medium. By logically connecting the transmit and receive lines, access to the medium becomes similar to that of an Ethernet interface; in fact, the interface becomes a pure bus medium interface, receiving what it sends.

The experiments were developed based upon the approach outlined by Reiss,[1] who created several experiments in assembly language to explain networking concepts. The experiments are cumulative, each using the steps completed by the previous experiments. The hardware setup can be found in Reiss. Many functions are written in assembly language,[2] for displaying the keyboard and network status as well as for transmitting/receiving the data to/from the network. However, these functions are transparent to the students. Students are only required to use the function calls in their programs written in C. This simplifies the programming task for CS students with no assembly-language background. The networking concepts covered are data framing and error checking, packet assembly/disassembly and addressing, CSMA/CD and Token Bus protocols.

---

[1] Reiss, Leszek (1987), *Introduction to Local Area Networks with Microcomputer Experiments*, Prentice Hall, Englewood Cliffs, NJ.
[2] These functions can be found on http://www.cps.cmich.edu/faculty/akhtar.

9

1.4 Asynchronous Byte (Character) Transfers

by

Shakil Akhtar

Objective: Explains how characters (bytes) transmit on the transmission line.

Brief Description: This experiment concentrates on elementary issues related to the use of terminal and network ports and asynchronous data transmission. From the data communication point of view, the experiment implements one-directional, point-to-point data transfers with the data frame limited to 1 byte (or character). No frame addressing needs to be implemented at this point.

Audience: Computer science seniors with a programming and mathematics background.

Equipment: Interface box to connect PC serial ports on Motorola 68000-based systems, PC serial port, interfaces and wires.

Duration: Two weeks in a 15-week semester.

PROCEDURE:

Two types of network nodes must be implemented: transmitter and receiver. The transmitter node must directly and unconditionally transmit all characters entered from its keyboard. The receiver node should accept every character appearing on the network bus and display it on its screen. Additionally, characters entered at the transmitter's keyboard should also be displayed (echoed) on the transmitter's screen. Since all bytes entered are to be transmitted immediately, there is no possibility of erasing or replacing a character once a key on the keyboard is pressed. If one transmitter and two or more receivers are operating at the same time, all characters sent to the network bus appear simultaneously on the screens of both receivers. If two or more transmitters are operating at the same time, there is a possibility of collisions. If this happens, the receiver(s) will receive distorted information.

There are some predefined subroutines you may use to either pass the keyboard information to the network or the network information to the screen. You need to type a command to install the network driver. This driver lets you use all the subroutines and sets the device number to 4. Make sure that, in your program, the device number (devnum) is set as 4. The algorithms for transmitter and receiver should be as follows:

Transmitter:
```
set devnum;
repeat forever
if char at the keyboard then get the char;
    transmit the char;
    print the char;
/* end of if statement */
/* end of repeat loop */
/* end of main */
```

Receiver:
```
set devnum;
repeat forever
if char at the network then get the char;
    print the char;
/* end of if statement */
/* end of repeat loop */
/* end of main */
```

DEMONSTRATIONS:

1. Type and send a single-line (and a multiple-line) text from the transmitter node to the receiver node.

2. Use three nodes on the network and demonstrate properties of bus topology (broadcast, contention and collision).

   a. Use one transmitter and two receivers (broadcast)

   b. Use two transmitters and one receiver (contention).

   c. Try to create collisions with two transmitters and one receiver.

Lab Report:

Include the program listing and details of all the demonstrations you carried out. Also, put enough comments in your program to make the code clear. You should include a flowchart in your report.

PART 2
DATA LINK LAYER

2.1 Data Frame Transfers

by

Shakil Akhtar

Objective: Explains how data frames are made and transmitted on the transmission line.

Brief Description: This experiment deals with transfers of data frames instead of single characters. Data consists of ASCII characters which are entered from the keyboard and embedded in a frame. A frame is obtained by adding headers and trailers to the raw data.

Audience: Computer science seniors with a programming and mathematics background.

Equipment: Interface box to connect PC serial ports on Motorola 68000-based systems, PC serial port, interfaces and wires.

Duration: Two weeks in a 15-week semester.

PROCEDURE:

The frame (or packet) format must be as follows:

```
PRE, data, EOT
```

where PRE is a front delimiter and EOT is an end delimiter. The PRE byte used is an all-zero byte (i.e., all bits are zeros). The EOT delimiter marks the end of a data frame. The binary code used for the EOT byte equals the ASCII code for EOT (i.e., $04). The character string in the data part should be limited to one line (or 80 characters), and during message input the CR key should be used to terminate the message. To provide for clarity of messages on terminal screens during both frame input and display, the last two characters of the data field should be the ASCII codes for CR (Carriage Return) and LF (Line Feed). Thus, the data field consists of:

```
character string, CR, LF
```

resulting in the following frame:

```
PRE, character string entered from the keyboard, CR,
LF, EOT
```

As long as there is only one transmitter on the network, there is no problem and everything goes smoothly. When there are two transmitters and one receiver, the frames are supposed to overlap, resulting in bad output at the receiver end. Make sure to provide a buffer space at the receiving end for storing the incoming frame from the network. Also, your program should be designed so that, as long as there is one frame in the receiving buffer, the node does not accept any other incoming frame. The collision may occur only when the frames are intermixed on the transmission line (and not in the receiving buffer). Note that, when there is only one transmitter and one receiver, there is no possibility of a collision. The algorithms for transmitter and receiver are as follows:

Transmitter:
```
set devnum;
repeat forever
if char at the keyboard then get the char;
    array [0] = PRE;
    while char != CR
        place char in the array;
        inc array index;
        get the char;
    /* while end */
place CR in array
inc array index
place LF in array
inc array index
place EOT in array
output frame to the network
/* char by char as in the previous experiment */
/* end of if statement */
/* end of repeat loop */
/* end of main */
```

Receiver:
```
set devnum;
repeat forever
if char at the network then get the char;
    if char = PRE then continue;
    while char<>EOT
    place in array;
    inc array index;
    get the char;
    /* while end */
    ignore PRE;
    output character string;
    ignore CR;
    ignore LF;
    ignore EOT;
 /* end of if statement */
 /* end of repeat loop */
 /* end of main */
```

DEMONSTRATIONS:

1. Enter and send a few one-line frames from the transmitter to the receiver node.

2. Use two receiver nodes and demonstrate a frame broadcast.

3. Use two transmitters and one receiver and send frames from the transmitters simultaneously. Explain the data that is displayed on the receiver's screen.

4. Change the PRE byte and demonstrate the effects of frame format mismatch by using one node as transmitter and one as receiver.

Lab Report:

Include the program listing and details of all the demonstrations you carried out. Also, put enough comments in your program to make the code clear. You should also include a flowchart of your program in your report.

2.2 Bidirectional Frame Transfers

by

Shakil Akhtar

Objective: Explains how bidirectional data is transmitted with implementations of application and network layer protocols

Brief Description: This experiment is an extension of the previous experiment. The same frame format is used. In this experiment, the transmitter and receiver codes are combined into one to allow bidirectional transfer (i.e., each node is capable of transmitting and receiving). Obviously, the complexity is increased due to the fact that stations can send at any time. If a message is received while the station is in the transmit mode, ignore the incoming message. Similarly, if a station is in the receive mode and a keyboard message is typed in, it should be ignored. As in the previous experiments, no provision for collision detection is provided. Therefore, collisions are expected. Some higher-level concepts are implemented. Special implementations at the network and application layers are considered with the help of several flags.

Audience: Computer science seniors with a programming and mathematics background.

Equipment: Interface box to connect PC serial ports on Motorola 68000-based systems, PC serial port, interfaces and wires.

Duration: Two weeks in a 15-week semester.

PROCEDURE:

The transmit buffer gets the input from the keyboard and transmits the data to the network bus. The receive buffer gets the data from the network, and the data is displayed on the screen. The function of each node is grouped into Application Layer (AL) and Network Layer (NL)[1] tasks. AL tasks are the user-level tasks, such as display of messages on the screen and input of messages from the keyboard. NL tasks are the ones closer to the network, such as communication of data. In AL, the defined states are ready, input and output. Ready state implies that flags are set in

---

[1] The (NL) and (AL) designations of this and the following experiments are designed to distinguish between the data in the packet format, as opposed to the data in the character format. Do not confuse them with the layers of the OSI model.

such a way that AL may switch to either the input state or the output state. In other words, if AL is ready and a key is pressed, the state change will occur to the input state. Similarly, if data is received from NL while AL is in the ready state, the state is changed to the output state. It should be noticed that no transition is allowed between input and output states. Therefore, while AL is in the input state it may only switch to the ready state after it has passed the data to NL.

At NL the states are ready, transmit and receive. When NL receives data from the network, it is considered to be in the receive state. Similarly, when it transmits the data to the network, it is in the transmit state. Again, notice that no direct transition between transmit and receive states is possible. Therefore, when a node is transmitting the data, it cannot receive any data until the end of the transmission, and when a node is receiving the data, it cannot transmit until the receiving is complete. We need to define some flags for communication between AL and NL. These flags may be used by one layer to indicate to another layer a change of states. For example, TF is defined as the "transmit flag" by AL to indicate to NL that a frame is ready and it must be transmitted. Similarly, DF may be defined as "display flag" by NL to AL, indicating that a message is ready to be displayed. Other flags may be used to show the states of NL and AL. The relationship between different state indicator flags is shown in the following table.

Table 2.1 NETWORK LAYER FLAGS

State	NR (Network Receiving)	NT (Network Transmitting)
Ready	0	0
Receive	1	0
Transmit	0	1

Table 2.2 APPLICATION LAYER FLAGS

State	AI (Application Inputting)	AD (Application Displaying)
Ready	0	0
Input	1	0
Output	0	1

Two more flags are defined for "transmit buffer full" and "receive buffer full" conditions (TBF and RBF). The defined flags, in conjunction with some other conditions, determine the functions of the AL and NL state machines. These other conditions indicate the status of the keyboard and/or network at any time. The function of each layer consists of taking some actions and setting up some other flags based upon the conditions. The final action taken by each node is either to put a frame on the network or get a frame from the network.

Table 2.3 FUNCTION OF AL STATE MACHINE

Current state	Next state	Condition	Action
Ready	Input	First char from keyboard and TBF == 0	AI = 1
Input	Ready	CR from keyboard	AI = 0, TF = 1, TBF = 1
Ready	Output	DF == 1	DF = 0, AD = 1
Output	Ready	Last character displayed	AD = 0, RBF = 0

Table 2.4 FUNCTION OF NL STATE MACHINE

Current state	Next state	Condition	Action
Ready	Receive	PRE received and RBF = 0	Receive NR = 1
Receive	Ready	EOT received	NR = 0, DF = 1, RBF = 1
Ready	Transmit	TF = 1	TF = 0, NT = 1
Transmit	Ready	EOT sent	NT = 0, TBF = 0

ALGORITHM FOR AL AND NL MACHINES:

```
set devnum;
init flags and variables;
repeat forever

/*  AL MACHINE  */

if char at the keyboard and TBF==0 then
    AI=1;
    get the char;
    array [0]=PRE;
    while char!=CR
        place char in the array;
        nc array index;
        get the char;
    /* while end */
    place CR in array;
    inc array index;
    place LF in array;
    inc array index;
    place EOT in array;
    AI=0; TF=1; TBF=1;
/* end of if statement */

if DF = 1 then
    DF = 0; AD = 1;
    get the char from buffer;
    display the char string until CR;
```

```
      ignore CR;
      ignore LF;
      ignore EOT;
      AD = 0; RBF = 0;
/* end of if statement */



/*    NL MACHINE    */

if char at the network and RBF==0 then
   NR=1;
     get the char;
   if char==PRE then continue;
   while char!=EOT
      place in array;
      inc array index;
      get the char;
   /* while end */
   NR=0; DF=1; RBF=1;
   /* end of if statement */

if TF = 1 then
   TF = 0; NT = 1;
   send char to the network until EOT;
   NT = 0; TBF = 0;
  /* end of if statement */
/* end of repeat loop */
/* end of main */
```

DEMONSTRATIONS:

1.   Enter and send a few one-line frames from a node to any other node.

2.   Use two nodes as receivers and demonstrate a frame broadcast.

3.   Use two nodes as transmitters and one as a receiver and send frames from the two transmitters simultaneously. Explain the data that is displayed on the receiver's screen.

Lab Report:

Include the program listing and details of all the demonstrations you carried out. Also put enough comments in your program to make the code clear. You should include a flowchart of your program in the report.

2.3 Addressed Frame Broadcast and Reception

by

Shakil Akhtar

Objective: Packet addressing using source/destination identification is explained.

Brief Description: This experiment is an extension of the previous one. The frame format is modified to handle addressed communication. At the start, every participating station sets up its own ID and then asks the user for an outgoing message. A packet is then formed using an approach similar to the previous experiments. As far as the receiver node is concerned, it is responsible for analyzing each incoming packet, and if the packet is not meant for it, discarding it.

Audience: Computer science seniors with a programming and mathematics background.

Equipment: Interface box to connect PC serial ports on Motorola 68000-based systems, PC serial port, interfaces and wires.

Duration: Two weeks in a 15-week semester.

PROCEDURE:

The modified packet version is shown below. It contains DID and SID (destination and source IDs, respectively), in addition to the packet format used for the previous experiments.

```
PRE, DID, SID ,...., data...., EOT
```

The transmitter code is modified to include the two new fields. When the packet is created using the AL software, these two fields may be inserted. One byte is reserved for each. The receiver is responsible for checking the incoming messages for the correct DID. Therefore, the NL code should be modified.

For this experiment, receive state is modified as three substates (R_0, R_1 and R_2). In state R_0, the node is expected to receive the PRE byte. Transition to state R_0 is possible from any state. As soon as the PRE byte is received, the transition is made to R_1 from R_0. The next byte expected is the DID. The node is supposed to compare DID with its own ID (i.e., My ID (MID)). If there is no match (DID! = MID) then the state transition is made to R_0, where the node waits for the next packet start (PRE). This loop is repeated until a match is found between DID and MID. Then the transition is made to R_2 instead of R_1. The exact condition for the transition would be DID = MID and RBF = 0. Recall that RBF is the flag used to indicate that the receive buffer is empty. The final transition is made from R_2 to R_0, indicating that the end of packet has reached (i.e., byte received = EOT). Now, the flags may be reset to start the reception of another packet. The three receive states could be indicated by a flag called RST. Its values of 0, 1 and 2 may signify the states R_0, R_1 and R_2 respectively.

DEMONSTRATIONS:

1. Enter and send a few one-line frames from one node to the other.

2. Use two nodes as receivers and demonstrate a frame broadcast.

3. Use two nodes as transmitters and one as receiver and send frames from the two transmitters simultaneously. Explain the data that is displayed on the receiver's screen.

Lab Report:

Include the program listing and details of all the demonstrations you carried out. Also, put enough comments in your program to make the code clear. You should include a flowchart and/or the algorithm in your report.

2.4 CSMA Medium-Access Scheme

by

Shakil Akhtar

Objective: Explains how the Carrier Sensing Multiple Access scheme is implemented on the serial port.

Brief Description: This experiment illustrates the concept of Carrier Sensing Multiple Access (CSMA) protocol used for local-area networks. The protocol suggests that a node should sense the medium before transmitting. A frame is transmitted only if the medium is free. The frame transmission is completed hoping that there are no collisions. Once the frame transmission starts, it is completed even if a collision occurs. This technique prevents the collisions to some extent but does not eliminate them completely. Thus, if two nodes start the transmission at almost the same time, a collision is likely to occur.

Audience: Computer science seniors with a programming and mathematics background.

Equipment: Interface box to connect PC serial ports on Motorola 68000-based systems, PC serial port, interfaces and wires.

Duration: Two weeks in a 15-week semester.

PROCEDURE:

The NL developed in the previous experiment is modified to implement the CSMA scheme. The same frame format is used and the messages are received exactly in the same manner. Only the transmitter part is modified.

Medium sensing is done by observing the medium in the receive direction for a limited amount of time A_t. If nothing is received during that period, it is assumed that the medium is free and the transmission is started. The medium speed is 19.2 kbps. With this speed, the time to transmit one byte would be $8/19200 = 0.4167$ msec. Allowing one byte time for the ACIA delay, a total waiting time of two bytes ($A_t = 0.8333$ msec) should be enough to detect any transmission on the medium. If the medium is found busy (i.e., if a character is found on the medium), the transmission is deferred and the medium sensing is repeated after two bytes time again.

The algorithm design is simple. Waiting can be achieved by introducing a meaningless loop with a high count value. The instruction performed in the loop may take a finite amount of time. If the medium is found busy, the NOP (no operation) loop can be entered and executed for 0.8333 msec. At the end, the medium is checked again. If the medium is still busy, the operation is repeated until it is found to be free. A flag called NFY can be used to indicate the status of the medium. If NFY is 0, the medium is busy; otherwise, it is free. The flag must be reset to 0 as soon as the PRE byte of a packet is received at a station.

DEMONSTRATIONS:

1. Enter and send a few one-line frames from one node to the other.

2. Use two nodes as receivers and demonstrate a frame broadcast.

3. Use two nodes as transmitters and one as a receiver and send frames from the two transmitters simultaneously. Explain the data that is displayed on the receiver's screen.

4. Explain which version of CSMA protocol is implemented.

Lab Report:

Include the program listing and details of all the demonstrations you carried out. Also, put enough comments in your program to make the code clear. You should include a flowchart and/or the algorithm in your report.

2.5 CSMA/CD Medium-Access Scheme

by

Shakil Akhtar

Objective: Explains how collision detection is implemented in a CSMA-based system.

Brief Objective: This experiment illustrates the concept of Carrier Sensing Multiple Access protocol with Collision Detection (CSMA/CD) used for local-area networks. It is an extension of the CSMA protocol. As soon as a collision is noticed, the transmitter aborts the transmission and retransmits after a random time interval. The protocol suggests that a node should sense the medium before transmitting. A frame is transmitted, only if the medium is free. The frame transmission is completed only if there is no collision. Using this technique, collisions are not noticed by the user. In other words, even if a collision takes place at the NL, the user is never going to notice it, since the frame retransmission is done at the NL.

Audience: Computer science seniors with a programming and mathematics background.

Equipment: Interface box to connect PC serial ports on Motorola 68000-based systems, PC serial port, interfaces and wires.

Duration: Two weeks in a 15-week semester.

PROCEDURE:

This experiment examines the situation of collision detection for CSMA (see the previous experiment). An additional piece of circuitry[1] is necessary for this experiment, as the collision can be detected only with two nodes outputing a signal level representing logical 0. By having an interrupt for this detector, it becomes possible to handle the collisions in the network. When a collision is detected, a transmitting node will inform the user of the situation and abort the transfer. If a receiving node detects a collision, it aborts the reception of the current frame and clears its input buffer. The retransmission of frames is not implemented, but by simply requeuing the packet, this can be accomplished. The algorithm for this experiment is unchanged for message creation and consumption, from the previous experiment. Af-

[1] See Reiss, Leszek (1987), *Introduction to Local Area Networks with Microcomputer Experiments*, Prentice Hall, Englewood Cliffs, NJ, for hardware setup.

ter a message has been created, its transmission begins immediately and unconditionally. However, should a collision occur during frame transmission, the transmission is aborted and the user is informed about it by a message appearing on the terminal screen. Since retransmissions are not implemented, if a collision occurs, the message is lost.

Medium sensing is done by observing the medium in receive direction for a limited amount of time A_t. If nothing is received during that period, it is assumed that the medium is free and the transmission is started. The medium speed is 19.2 kbps. With this speed, the time to transmit one byte would be $8/19200 = 0.4167$ msec. Allowing one byte time for the ACIA (serial port) delay, a total waiting time of two bytes ($A_t = 0.8333$ msec) should be enough as a minimum waiting time before transmission. In other words, each station senses the medium for two bytes time, and if the medium is free, it transmits. This is carrier sensing as done in the previous experiment.

To implement CSMA/CD, check the status of the medium before transmission. If the medium is found free, do not transmit right away. Wait for two bytes time and then check the medium again. If the medium is again free, then start the transmission. When the medium is found busy in carrier sensing, a station must defer for a random amount of time. That random time must be greater than two bytes time, which is the minimum duration for carrier sensing. The maximum random value could be as much as 20 to 30 bytes time.

In CSMA protocol, once the frame transmission starts, it does not stop due to collision, whereas in CSMA/CD protocol, the transmission is aborted as soon as a collision is noticed. The hardware implementation in the lab allows for the collision detection, since every station can receive the transmission. Once the transmitter starts, it can compare its transmit buffer to what it sees on the medium. If it finds only its own characters on the medium, there is no collision. In the event of no collision, the station continues until there is either a collision (station detects garbage on the medium) or the packet ends.

Again, in this experiment, waiting can be achieved by introducing a meaningless loop with a high count value. The instruction performed in the loop will take a finite amount of time. If the medium is found busy, the NOP (no operation) loop can be entered and executed for two bytes time (0.8333 msec). At the end, the medium is checked again. If the medium is still busy, the operation is repeated after a random period of time until it is found to be free. A flag called NFY can be used by network layer to indicate the status of the medium. If NFY is 0, the medium is busy; otherwise it is free. The flag must be reset to 0 as soon as the PRE byte of a packet is received at a receiving station. The complete CSMA/CD algorithm is given below:

```
/* AL Machine */
repeat forever
if char at the keyboard and TBF == 0 then
  AI = 1;
  get the char;
  array[0] = PRE;
  get the next char;
  if char = machine ID then   /* check address */
```

```
  while char != CR
     place char in the array;
     inc array index;
     get the char;
  /* end while */
 place CR in array;
 inc array index;
 place LF in array;
 inc array index;
 place EOT in array;
 AI = 0; TF = 1; TBF = 1;
/* end of if statements */
if DF == 1 then
  DF = 0; AD = 1;
  get the char from buffer;
  display the char string until CR;
  ignore CR;
  ignore LF;
  ignore EOT;
  AD = 0; RBF = 0;
/* end of if statement */

/* NL Machine */
if char at the network and RBF == 0 then
  NBY = 0;              /* assume that the network medium is
                        /* free */
  wait 2 byte times;/* loop */
  if NBY == 0 then     /* if medium is still free */
    BYS = 1;           /* enter transmit state */
    SP = 0;            /* clear packet transmission
                        /* request */
  else
    wait for a random amount of time (greater than
      2 bytes time);
  /* end of if statement */
  NR = 1;
  get the char;
  if char = PRE then continue;
  while char != EOT
    place in array;
    inc array index;
    get the char;
  /* end while */
  NR = 0; DF = 1; RBF = 1;
 /* end of if statement */
if TF == 1 then
  TF = 0; NT = 1;
  while not EOT
    send char from transmit buffer to network;
    compare contents of buffer with the characters on
      the network;
    if correct seq of chars is on the net, continue trm.
    else abort transmission;  /* as this implies
                               /* collision */
```

```
      /* end while */
      NT = 0; TBF = 0;
   /* end of if statement */
   /* end of repeat loop */
   /* end of main */
```

DEMONSTRATIONS:

1. Enter and send a few one-line frames from one node to the other.

2. Use two nodes as receivers and demonstrate a frame broadcast.

3. Use two nodes as transmitters and one as receiver and send frames from two transmitters simultaneously. Explain the data that is displayed on the receiver's screen. Is a collision taking place?

4. Explain which version is implemented in the CSMA part of the CSMA/CD protocol.

Lab Report:

Include the program listing and details of all the demonstrations you carried out. Also, put enough comments in your program to make the code clear. You should include a flowchart and/or the algorithm in your report.

2.6 Token-Bus Medium-Access Scheme

by

Shakil Akhtar

Objective: Explains how a token-passing scheme is implemented on a bus-based system.

Brief Objective: This experiment illustrates the operation of a token-bus LAN. The scope of the protocol is limited and does not include token recovery or network reconfiguration operations. Since token recovery is not supported, a loss of token stops the network operation.

Audience: Computer science seniors with a programming and mathematics background.

Equipment: Interface box to connect PC serial ports on Motorola 68000-based systems, PC serial port, interfaces and wires.

Duration: Two weeks in a 15-week semester.

PROCEDURE:

This experiment introduces the token-bus medium-access scheme. A token-bus logical ring is implemented using two types of frames—the normal frame as outlined in the Addressed Frame Broadcast and Reception Experiment, and a "token" frame containing only the destination address. Thus the token frame format is: PRE, DID, EOT. This experiment deals with sending and receiving the token: when a token is sent to a successor, the transmitting node waits for a response. It does not implement any token recovery, so if the token is lost, the network operations halt. The network also needs to be started manually by an operator, since no ring initialization procedure is included. The AL is still unchanged for this experiment. The NL, however, has the following states: receive, send packet and send token. In the receive state, the NL monitors the frames arriving from the network medium and awaits a token or packet frame. If a packet is received, the application layer is informed about it, but the NL remains in the receive state, ready to accept another packet or the token frame. If the token is received, it means that the node obtained the right to transmit. If a packet is waiting to be transmitted, the state is changed to send packet, and transmission begins. The request to send a packet is signaled in the application-network interlayer interface by a flag. After packet

29

transmission has been completed, the state is changed to send token, and token transmission begins. The algorithm for this experiment follows:

```
/* AL Machine */
repeat forever
if char at the keyboard and TBF == 0 then
  AI = 1;
  get the char;
  array[0] = PRE;
  get the next char;
  if char == machine ID then /* check address */
  while char != CR
    place char in the array;
    inc array index;
    get the char;
  /* end while */
  if token sequence has been received
    set token received flag to 1;
    display message "Token Received....";
  else
    place CR in array;
    inc array index;
    place LF in array;
    inc array index;
    place EOT in array;
    AI = 0; TF = 1; TBF = 1;
/* end of if statements */
if DF == 1 then
  DF = 0; AD = 1;
  get the char from buffer;
  display the char string until CR;
  ignore CR;
  ignore LF;
  ignore EOT;
  AD = 0; RBF = 0;
/* end of if statement */

/* NL Machine */
if char at the network and RBF == 0 then
  NR = 1;
  get the char;
  if char == PRE then continue;
  while char != EOT
    place in array;
    inc array index;
    get the char;
  /* end while */
  NR = 0; DF = 1; RBF = 1;
/* end of if statement */
if (TF == 1 and token received flag set to 1) then
  TF = 0; NT = 1;
  send char to network until EOT;
  NT = 0; TBF = 0;
```

```
/* end of if statement */
/* end of repeat loop */
/* end of main */
```

DEMONSTRATIONS:

1. Enter and send a few one-line frames between various nodes.

2. Use two nodes as receivers and demonstrate a frame broadcast.

3. Use two nodes as transmitters and one as receiver and send frames from the two transmitters simultaneously. Is there a collision taking place? If not, why?

4. Explain why the display is different from the previous experiment, even when the frames are transmitted simultaneously.

Lab Report:

Include the program listing and details of all the demonstrations you carried out. Also, put enough comments in your program to make the code clear. You should include a flowchart and/or the algorithm in your report.

2.7 Simulation of Simplex Stop-and-Wait with PAR

by

Peter Sanderson

Objective: This programming exercise will help you understand data link transmission protocols for noisy simplex channels, by simulating the simplex stop-and-wait protocol with positive acknowledgment and retransmission (PAR).

Brief Description: This exercise will simulate the simplex stop-and-wait protocol with positive acknowledgment and retransmission (PAR). Simplex protocols for noisy channels are described on pages 197–202 of Tanenbaum's[1] *Computer Networks* (third edition). The program will "transmit" the contents of an ASCII data file. The basic solution requires a transmitter function, a receiver function, checksum functions, and a gremlin function (to create errors). These functions can be implemented either in a single program or as multiple programs communicating through pipes. An example single program solution follows. The transmitter reads data from the file, creates the data frame, calculates the checksum, applies the gremlin, then calls the receiver. The receiver checks the checksum, writes the correct frame to the output file, and returns the acknowledgment. This assignment requires a substantial design and programming effort and should be solved by teams of two students.

Audience: This laboratory exercise comes from the upper-division undergraduate elective course Theory of Telecommunications. Its prerequisite is the Data Structures course. It is intended mainly for computer science majors having a strong mathematics and physics background. It is also recommended for computer information systems majors who have taken a networks course and desire a more in-depth study of networking fundamentals.

Equipment required: None. This simulation exercise can be programmed using any available language. The advanced solution requires interprocess communication techniques normally covered in an operating-systems course.

Duration: Two weeks.

---

[1] Professors may find the corresponding pages in their own texts.

PROCEDURE:

In this assignment you will simulate the simplex stop-and-wait protocol with positive acknowledgment and retransmission (PAR). Use the language or compiler of your choice. You may work either individually or with a partner.

The problem itself is straightforward. The simplex stop-and-wait with PAR is covered on pages 197–202 of the Tanenbaum text, and the algorithms for both sender and receiver are specified in Figure 3-11 of that text. Of course, the program cannot just be typed in as is and run. For one thing, the sender and receiver would have to be two separately running processes which can nevertheless communicate with each other as necessary. For another, the algorithm contains a timing mechanism and event waiting.

The solution described here does not require concurrency. If you know how to write programs which can be run as separate processes and communicate via pipes, I encourage you to pursue that solution strategy instead of the one outlined here. If you want an even greater challenge, implement a full solution which handles lost frames and uses timers and signals for acknowledgment.

The goal is to simulate the transmission of an ASCII file. The sender will read from the file (network layer) and transmit its contents to the receiver, which will write the information to another file (network layer). Filenames are entered at runtime.

The data link protocol implemented in your program must provide the network layer an error-free, sequenced transmission service. The input stream will be broken up by your program into frames. It will transmit the frames one by one according to the protocol. It will reconstruct the data stream at the other end and write it to the file.

This solution simplifies the algorithm by not requiring the timing mechanism or event waiting. Data frames may be damaged but not lost. The sender and receiver are two separate functions.

The sender is given a stream of input data. It will break the data into data frames of eight bytes. If the total length is not a multiple of eight, pad the last frame with 0s. If the total length *is* a multiple of eight, make the last data frame all 0s. This should be recognized on the receiving side as the end of the file. Each frame will also have a 16-bit checksum attached, using CRC coding based on the CRC-CCITT generator polynomial. The frame is now 10 bytes in length (eight bytes data plus two bytes CRC). The most advanced solution requires a one-bit sequence number, which can be added as a one-byte field to the frame structure. The others do not require sequence because frames are not lost or delivered out of order.

The frame will first be passed to a gremlin function, which will occasionally damage the frame (this simulates transmission errors). The result is then "sent" to the receiver function. The sender then waits for ACK or NAK from the receiver. ACK means "The frame was received OK, so send the next." NAK means "The frame was damaged, please send again." The sender gets ACK/NAK as the return value of the receiver function. ACK/NAKs are never damaged or lost.

The receiver will read each frame. It must first check for checksum errors. If no error occurred, it will return an ACK to the sender. Otherwise, it will return a

NAK to request retransmission. Use any values you wish to represent ACK/NAK. It is the receiver's responsibility to reassemble frames into an output stream.

The gremlin function uses a random-number generator to determine whether to damage a frame, and, if so, how many and which bits to flip. The probability that a given frame will be damaged, P(d), will be entered at runtime. If the frame is to be damaged, the probability of flipping one bit is .5, the probability of flipping two bits is .3, and the probability of flipping three bits is .2. Every bit in the frame is equally likely to be damaged.

Include a trace option for both the sender and the receiver. If trace is on, the sender will output the message:

```
Frame xxx transmitted -- yyy.
```

where **xxx** is the frame number (just maintain a counter of frames successfully transmitted), and **yyy** is the string either "intact" or "damaged." depending on whether the gremlin damages it or not. The receiver will likewise output the message:

```
Frame xxx received -- yyy.
```

with the analogous meanings. The trace option is specified at runtime.

PROGRAM INPUT FROM USER:

1. Name of input file

2. Name of output file

3. Probability that a frame will be damaged

4. Whether or not frame tracing should be enabled

PROGRAM OUTPUT TO SCREEN (AFTER TRANSMISSION COMPLETE):

1. Total number of packets read from sender's network layer

2. Total number of frames transmitted (correct plus damaged)

3. Total number of frames damaged

4. Maximum number of retransmissions for any single frame

5. Total number of packets delivered to receiver's network layer

Lab Report:

The report should include source and executable files.

2.8 Cyclic Redundancy Check (CRC) Generating and Receiving Circuits

by

Essaid Bouktache

Objective: The objective of this lab is to implement circuits that generate and receive CRC codes for error detection using linear shiftback registers, and to verify their functionality by comparing these hardware-generated codes with the ones computed using polynomial division.

Brief Description: CRC code generation is an important tool in computer networking at the data link layer level, since it is at that level that error detection is done by hardware. At a higher layer (transport), error detection is done in software, using a much simpler algorithm to allow speedy processing. In all cases, error detection provides an efficient means of implementing error control for reliable transmission of messages.

Audience: Undergraduate students with a minimum knowledge of digital and sequential logic.

Equipment Per Station:
- $1 \times$ "Digi-Designer" with breadboard, debounced switches and LEDs.
- 2×7474 (D flip-flops).
- 1×7486 (exclusive OR gates).
- Breadboard wires.

Duration: Three hours.

PROCEDURE:

PRELIMINARIES

1. Polynomial Arithmetic for CRC Generation:

The CRC, or frame check sequence **R**, is the remainder of the following binary division: $2^n \times$ **M/P**. **M** is a k-bit message and **P** is a generating polynomial of degree **n**. Generating polynomials, also called prime polynomials, are listed in textbooks on coding theory. The remainder **R** is then appended to the message **M** to form a **(k + n)**-bit frame **T** to be transmitted.

2. Polynomial Arithmetic for CRC Reception:

At the receiver, the received frame **T** is divided by the same generating polynomial **P**. A remainder of 0 indicates no error. Any other remainder is an indication of a burst error. Codes that are generated using shiftback registers and based on generating polynomials can detect 100% of all burst errors up to length **n**, that is, up to **n** bits in error, where **n** is the degree of the generating polynomial **P**. Higher burst lengths can also be detected, but at a lesser percentage.

3. A Working Example:

Using modulo-2 polynomial arithmetic, find the CRC to be appended to the message M = 11100110, given the generating polynomial $P(X) = X^4 + X^3 + 1$.

PROCEDURE:

1. P(X) is a 4th-degree polynomial, hence **n = 4**.

2. Write the message M in polynomial form: $M(X) = X^7 + X^6 + X^5 + X^2 + X$.

   (The rightmost bit in M is the weight for X^0, the next bit is the weight for X^1, etc.)

3. Perform the following long division: $2^n \times M/P = X^4 M(X)/P(X)$, since n = 4.

$$\frac{X^4 M(X)}{P(X)} = \frac{X^{11} + X^{10} + X^9 + X^6 + X^5}{X^4 + X^3 + 1}$$

   Note: In modulo-2 arithmetic, a subtraction is the same as an addition; for example, subtracting $X^8 + X^7 + X^4$ from $X^8 + X^7 + X^6$ will result in $X^6 + X^4$, and adding $X^8 + X^8$ will give 0, etc.

4. The remainder of the long division is $R(X) = X^2 + X = 0\ 1\ 1\ 0$, which must have four bits, since n = 4.

5. The frame to be transmitted is T = 1 1 1 0 0 1 1 0 0 1 1 0, that is, the message M immediately followed by the CRC, which is 0110.

6. In order to check for errors at the receiver, perform a long division of T(X) by P(X). For the error-free frame, $T(X) = X^{11} + X^{10} + X^9 + X^6 + X^5 + X^2 + X$, and the remainder R(X) is 0.

7. For this particular example, all errors of up to four bits in the received frame T can be detected, resulting in a nonzero R(X).

4. Hardware Circuit for Generation and Reception:

- The circuit is constructed using D flip-flops and exclusive-OR gates.

- The number of flip-flops is four, since n = 4, the degree of the generating polynomial P(X).

- General circuit for a 4-flip-flop register based on the following P(X):

```
P(X)  =  X⁴ + aX³ + bX² + cX + 1
```

where a, b, or c are 1 for feedback, and 0 for no feedback.

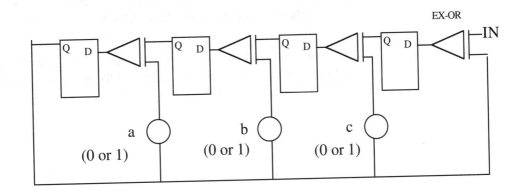

CIRCUIT #1

1. Use polynomial arithmetic to compute the CRC code which will be sent along with the following 12-bit message: $M = 1\ 1\ 0\ 0\ 1\ 1\ 1\ 0\ 1\ 0\ 1\ 1$. The generating polynomial is $P(X) = X^4 + X + 1$.

2. Using the provided hardware, build the shiftback register circuit which will generate the CRC code based on the above polynomial. Connect an LED to the output of each flip-flop.

3. Using the message M given above as an input to your circuit, apply the appropriate number of clock pulses (number of bits in M + n) to generate the CRC code, then compare with the result found using polynomial division. (Remember, you must apply the exact number of clock pulses.) *The first bit to be applied to the circuit is the leftmost bit of the message.* Use the push-button (which must be debounced) on the Digi-Designer as a manual clock. If you are using a plain push-button, you must add a debounce circuit or your code will be erroneous.

4. Clear the circuit so that all LEDs are off.

5. To verify that the circuit is working properly, first apply the received frame (frame = message followed by CRC code) with no errors. If your circuit is working as desired, the shift register should show *all zeros* at the end of the last clock pulse.

6. Again clear the circuit so that all LEDs are off.

7. a) This time assume that an error burst occurred *within the message bits* so that the message portion of the received frame is $Mr = 1\ 1\ 1\ 1\ 0\ 0\ 1\ 0\ 1\ 0\ 1\ 1$ instead of $1\ 1\ 0\ 0\ 1\ 1\ 1\ 0\ 1\ 0\ 1\ 1$. *Assume no errors in the received CRC code.* Show that your circuit can detect this error; i.e., the register contents (remainder) *should not be zero. Write down this remainder.*

   b) Perform the polynomial division using the information of question a) and compare with the code shown at the output of the flip-flops.

8. Repeat question 7 by introducing two errors in the message portion and two errors in the CRC code of the received frame.

CIRCUIT #2

Repeat Part II to verify the circuit used in the working example of part I-3 above which uses the generating polynomial $P(X) = X^4 + X^3 + 1$ and the message M = 1 1 1 0 0 1 1 0.

For question 7 of Part II, assume four errors in the message portion of the received frame and none in the CRC code, and for question 8, assume four errors in the CRC and none in the message.

2.9 Sliding Window Protocol

by

Ann Burroughs

Objective: To understand the sliding window protocol in terms of its flow-control and error-detection/correction features.

Brief Description: Following a textual scenario, students graphically represent the states of the sliding windows on either side of a communication process.

Audience: Students in data communications, telecommunications or networking who have had a lecture-mode introduction to the sliding window protocol.

Equipment: None. It may be helpful to look at a ShockWave animation of the sliding window protocol at www.humboldt.edu/~aeb3/SlidingWindow.html. This animation requires a ShockWave plug-in to the Web Browser.

Duration: One week.

PROCEDURE:

The objective of this exercise is to gain a better understanding of the working of the sliding window protocol for flow control and error detection. You might want to look at the sliding window protocol animation before you attempt to complete this exercise.

Complete the visual scenario from the written scenario, showing the effect of each event on the sender's window, the receiver's window, and the communications channel.

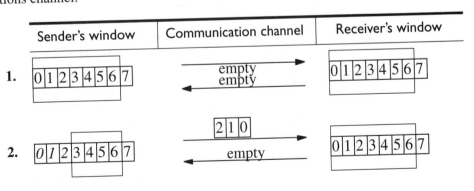

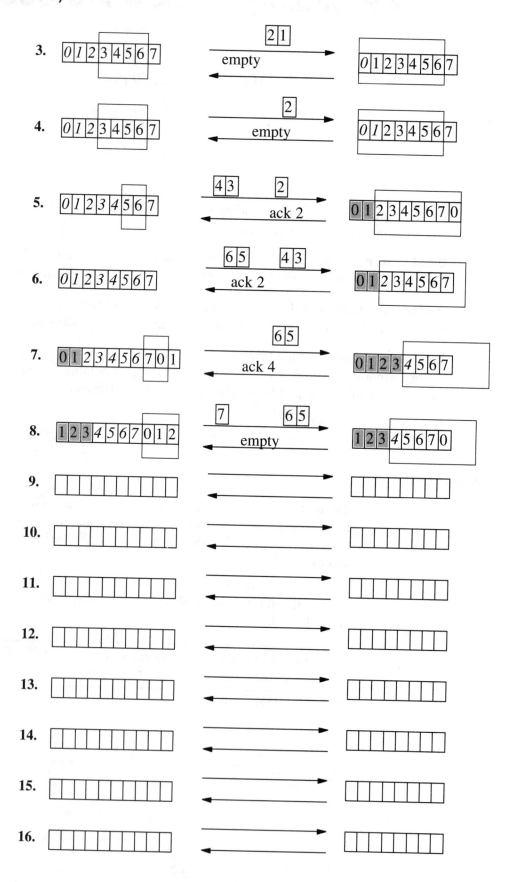

17. ⬚⬚⬚⬚⬚⬚⬚   →   ⬚⬚⬚⬚⬚⬚
          ←

18. ⬚⬚⬚⬚⬚⬚⬚   →   ⬚⬚⬚⬚⬚⬚
          ←

19. ⬚⬚⬚⬚⬚⬚⬚   →   ⬚⬚⬚⬚⬚⬚
          ←

20. ⬚⬚⬚⬚⬚⬚⬚   →   ⬚⬚⬚⬚⬚⬚
          ←

21. ⬚⬚⬚⬚⬚⬚⬚   →   ⬚⬚⬚⬚⬚⬚
          ←

22. ⬚⬚⬚⬚⬚⬚⬚   →   ⬚⬚⬚⬚⬚⬚
          ←

Scenario of events for communication between sender and receiver using sliding window protocol with a window size 7.

You can follow events 1 through 8 on the diagram. Note these conventions:

a. Sliding window opening indicated by   ——————→   ⬚

b. On sender side, frames sent but not yet acknowledged are *italicized*.

c. On receiver side, frames received but not yet acknowledged are *italicized*.

d. On sender and receiver side, frames which have been acknowledged are shaded. This is to show that they have been dealt with and are no longer interesting to the protocol, although a few of the most recently acknowledged frames are shown just for the sake of comprehension.

e. Data and control information is shown on the communication channel if it has been sent by either the sender or receiver and not yet received at the opposite end. Otherwise the communication channel is empty.

1. Sender has not yet sent any frame.

2. Sender has just sent frames 0, 1 and 2. Its window closes. Frames 0, 1 and 2 have been sent but not acknowledged.

3. Frame 0 has just arrived at receiver. It has been received but not yet acknowledged.

4. Frame 1 has just arrived at receiver. It has been received but not yet acknowledged.

5. Sender has just sent frames 3 and 4. Its window closes further. Frames 0, 1, 2, 3 and 4 have been sent but no acknowledgment has yet been received. Receiver has just acknowledged frames 0 and 1. Its window slides forward.

6. Frame 2 has just arrived at receiver. It has been received but not yet acknowledged. Sender has just sent frames 5 and 6. Frames 0 through 6 have been sent but no acknowledgment yet received. Sender's window is closed.

7. Acknowledgment for frames 0 and 1 has just been received by sender. Its window slides open two frames. Frames 3 and 4 have just arrived at receiver. Receiver has just acknowledged frames 2 and 3. Frame 4 has been received but not acknowledged. Receiver's window slides forward.

8. Acknowledgment for frames 2 and 3 has just been received by sender. Its window slides open two frames. Sender has just sent frame 7, sliding its window closed one frame. Frames 4, 5, 6 and 7 have been sent, but no acknowledgment has yet been received.

For each of the following events, represent the effect by showing it on the corresponding diagram.

9. Sender sends frame 0.

10. Frame 5 gets corrupted and cannot be interpreted at the receiver. Receiver acknowledges frame 4.

11. Sender sends frame 1. Sender receives acknowledgment for frame 4, which slides its window open one frame. Receiver receives frames 6, 7 and 0, which it must discard because it has not yet received frame 5. Receiver sends another acknowledgment for frame 4.

12. Sender's time-out clock for waiting for acknowledgment for frame 5 expires. Sender sends frames 5, 6, 7, 0 and 1 again, and also frame 2. Receiver receives frame 1 which it must discard because it has not yet received frame 5.

13. Sender receives the second acknowledgment for frame 4, which it discards because it has already received such an acknowledgment. Receiver receives frames 5, 6 and 7 and responds by acknowledging them all at once.

14. Receiver receives frame 0. The acknowledgment sent at moment 13 is destroyed by corruption.

15. Receiver receives frames 1 and 2. Receiver acknowledges frame 0.

16. Sender sends frame 3. Receiver acknowledges frames 1 and 2.

17. Sender's time-out for waiting for acknowledgment for frame 5 expires. Sender resends frames 5, 6, 7, 0, 1, 2 and 3.

18. Sender receives acknowledgment for frame 0 (don't forget that this is also an implicit acknowledgment for all unacknowledged frames prior to frame 0). Sender receives acknowledgment for frames 1 and 2. Receiver receives frame 3. Receiver receives resent frames 5, 6 and 7 (but since it is expecting frame __?__ it discards them).

19. Sender sends frames 4 and 5. Receiver receives resent frames 0, 1, 2 and 3. Receiver acknowledges frame 3.

20. Sender sends frames 6, 7, 0 and 1. Receiver receives frame 4.

21. Sender receives acknowledgment for frame 3. Receiver receives frames 5, 6 and 7.

22. Sender sends frame 2. Receiver receives frames 0 and 1. Receiver acknowledges frame 5.

PART 3
CLIENT/SERVER COMPUTING__ NETWORK AND TRANSPORT LAYERS

3.1 Introduction to Client/Server Message Passing in the TCP/IP UNIX and Internet Domains

by

Ted Mims

Objective: The purpose of this lab is to provide students with an introduction to sending and receiving data between processes in the UNIX and Internet domains. In a UNIX system, messages are sent and received over sockets as bytes. In order to send data that is not of type char, casting must be used. Students will get hands-on experience sending messages of different types and lengths between processes.

Brief Description: This module introduces students to the message-passing facilities utilized in the client/server example using the TCP/IP protocol for the UNIX and Internet domains. After completing the associated laboratory exercises the students will be able to distribute data of various types between processes that are distributed across a network. These laboratory exercises have been utilized by students in a first course in UNIX network programming. The students' anxiety level was reduced by allowing them to work through the exercises and providing them with the initial example from which to work.

Audience: Students who are learning the concepts related to the client/server model for processes communicating over a network. They should have a working knowledge of C and UNIX, and a basic understanding of the system calls socket, bind, listen, accept, select, read, write and close for using sockets.

Equipment: A UNIX system that will support the TCP/IP UNIX and Internet domains, and most graphics workstations, including those by HP, SUN, Silicon Graphics, NeXT, and DEC. PCs running the Linux operating system also provide an appropriate platform.

Duration: Three weeks.

PROCEDURE:

LABORATORY EXERCISE I

There are three sample programs located in files client1.c, client2.c and server.c.[1] The program client1.c passes a message of type character to the server.c process. The server process receives the character, increments it to the next letter in the al-

---

[1] These files are found at the end of this laboratory.

phabet, and sends the character to the client2.c process. The client2.c process receives the value from the server and prints it, and all the processes terminate. The processes are connected in a logical pipeline. You are to compile and execute this program using the UNIX domain first and the Internet domain second.

Lab Report:

a. Write a fully documented source listing of the three programs. You should add comments to explain how the socket system calls are being used.

b. Indicate the output from the client2 program. Run the program three times, using a different initial value for the character being sent from client1.

LABORATORY EXERCISE 2

Modify the program from laboratory exercise 1 so that it will send an integer value from client1 through the pipeline. The server process should increment the value by 1 and print it before passing it to the next process. Client2 should print the value it receives from the server.

Lab Report:

a. Write a fully documented source listing of the three programs. You should add comments to explain how the socket system calls are being used.

b. Indicate the output from server and client2 programs. Run the program three times using a different initial value for the integer being sent from client1.

c. Explain how you modified the program from exercise 1 so that integer values, rather than character messages, could be passed between processes.

LABORATORY EXERCISE 3

Modify the program from laboratory exercise 1 so that it will send a float value from client1 through the pipeline. The server process should increment the value by 0.5 and print it before passing it to the next process. Client2 should print the value it receives from the server.

Lab Report:

a. Write a fully documented source listing of the three programs. You should add comments to explain how the socket system calls are being used.

b. Indicate the output from server and client2 programs. Run the program three times using a different initial value for the float value being sent from client1.

c. Explain how you modified the program from exercise 1 so that float values, rather than character messages, could be passed between processes.

LABORATORY EXERCISE 4

Modify the program from laboratory exercise 1 so that it will send a message that is a structure containing values of type character, integer and float from the master through the pipeline. The server process should print the message using the format "char value %c integer value %d float value %f" before passing it to the next process. The server should change the value of each element of the structure before passing it to client2. Client2 should print the structure values it receives from the server using the above format.

Lab Report:

a. Write a fully documented source listing of the three programs. You should add comments to explain how the socket system calls are being used.

b. Indicate the output from server and client2 programs. Run the program three times using a different initial value for the float value being sent from client1.

c. Explain how you modified the program from exercise 1 so that structures, rather than character messages, could be passed between processes.

LABORATORY EXERCISE 5

Implement laboratory exercise 4 to run in the Internet domain. If the machine architectures are not the same, and if they do not all have the same size for your structure, you may have to design an algorithm for sending the structure.

Lab Report:

a. Write a fully documented source listing of the three programs. You should add comments to explain how the socket system calls are being used.

b. Indicate the output from server and client2 programs. Run the program three times using a different initial value for the float value being sent from client1.

c. Explain how you modified the program from exercise 4 so that it would run in the Internet domain.

```
/* -----------------client1.c-------------------- */

/* Written by Ted Mims

   Computer Science Department
   University of Illinois at Springfield
   PO Box 19243
   Springfield, IL 62794
   email mims.ted@uis.edu http://www.uis.edu/ ~mims */

/* This is the first client and it sends a character to
the server. The server must be running first.        */

#include <stdio.h>
#include <sys/types.h>
#include <sys/socket.h>
#include <sys/un.h>

/* err.c is a file that contains code for handling error
   messages and must be in the same directory as client1.c
   when client1.c is compiled.                          */

#include "err.c"
#define sname "socket1"
```

```
#define TRUE 1
#define FALSE 0

main ()
{
  int sd;
  typedef struct _msg

      {
        char char_value;
      } structure_type;
     structure_type structure;
   struct sockaddr_un name;
     /* create a socket for connecting to the server */
       sd = socket(AF_UNIX, SOCK_STREAM, 0);
       /* create a UNIX domain name                   */
       name.sun_family = AF_UNIX;
       strcpy(name.sun_path, sname);
       /* establish a connection to this name from
          created socket                              */
       if (connect(sd,&name, sizeof(name)) == -1)
          syserr("client-connect");
       /* initialize the character value to A         */
       structure.char_value = 'A';
       /* write the character to the socket           */
       write(sd, &structure, sizeof(structure));
       exit();
}

/* ------------------client2.c-------------------- */

/* Written by Ted Mims
   Computer Science Department
   University of Illinois at Springfield
   PO Box 19243
   Springfield, IL  62794
   email mims.ted@uis.edu  http://www.uis.edu/ ~mims */

/* This is the second client and it reads a character from
   the server.  The server must be running first.
*/

#include <stdio.h>
#include <sys/types.h>
#include <sys/socket.h>
#include <sys/un.h>
#include <sys/time.h>

/* err.c is a file that contains code for handling error
   messages and must be in the same directory as client2.c
   when client2.c is compiled.                          */
#include "err.c"
#define sname "socket1"
```

```c
#define TRUE 1
#define FALSE 0

main ()
{

    int sd;
    typedef struct _msg
        {
           char char_value;
        } structure_type;
       structure_type structure;
    struct sockaddr_un name;
        /* create a socket for connecting to the server */
        sd = socket(AF_UNIX, SOCK_STREAM, 0);
        /* create a UNIX domain name               */
        name.sun_family = AF_UNIX;
        strcpy(name.sun_path, sname);
        /* establish a connection to this name from
           created socket                          */
        if (connect(sd,&name, sizeof(name)) == -1)
          syserr("client-connect");
        /* initialize the character value to A      */
        read(sd, &structure, sizeof(structure));
      printf("\nThe value stored in structure is below\n");
       printf(" %c \n", structure.char_value);
        /* remove the socket using unlink socket     */
        unlink(sname);
        exit(0);
}


/* ----------------- server.c -------------------- */

/* Written by Ted Mims
   Computer Science Department
   University of Illinois at Springfield
   PO Box 19243
   Springfield, IL  62794
   email mims.ted@uis.edu  http://www.uis.edu/ ~mims */


   /* This is the server that reads a character from
      client1.c from the socket. The server will write the
      character to the socket and send it to client2.c
*/

#include <stdio.h>
#include <sys/types.h>
#include <sys/socket.h>
#include <sys/un.h>
#include <sys/time.h>
#include "err.c"
#define sname "socket1"
```

```
main ()
{
  int readable();
  int waitread();
  int sd, ns1, ns2, lin, is_ns_ready;

  typedef struct _msg
      {
       char char_value;
      } structure_type;
      structure_type structure;
  struct sockaddr_un name, namein;
  /* create socket for requests */
  sd = socket(AF_UNIX, SOCK_STREAM, 0);
  /* create a UNIX domain name */
  name.sun_family = AF_UNIX;
  strcpy(name.sun_path, sname);

  /* bind it to the created socket, and set max
  /* queue length */
  if (bind(sd, &name, sizeof(name)) != 0) syserr
      ("server-bind");
  listen(sd,5);
      /* accept a connection */
      namein.sun_family = AF_UNIX;
      strcpy(namein.sun_path, sname);
      lin = sizeof(namein);
      if ((ns1 = accept(sd, &namein, &lin)) == -1)
        syserr("ns-error");
      if ((ns2 = accept(sd, &namein, &lin)) == -1)
        syserr("ns-error");
      /* close sd - use only ns */
      close(sd);
      /* check to see if there is data to read on
        the socket */
      is_ns_ready = 0;
      while (is_ns_ready == 0)
  {
          is_ns_ready = readable(ns1);
          printf("is_ns_ready %d\n", is_ns_ready);
      }
    read(ns1, &structure, sizeof(structure));
  printf("\nThe value stored in structure is below\n");
    printf(" %c \n", structure.char_value);
    write(ns2, &structure, sizeof(structure));
    /* main server closes ns */
    close(ns1);
    close(ns2);
  exit(0);
}
/*
```

```
**  The following code was written by Steven Grimm
**  (koreth@ebay.sun.com) on 11-26-87
*/
/*
**  readable()
**
**  Poll a socket for pending input.  Returns immediate-
ly.
**  This is a front-end to waitread() below.
**
**  Input: file descriptor to poll
**  Output: 1 if data is available for reading
*/
int readable(fd)
int fd;
{
  return(waitread(fd, 0));
}


/*
**  waitread()
**
**  Wait for data on a file descriptor for a little while.
**
**  Input: file descriptor to watch
**    how long to wait, in seconds, before returning
**  Output: 1 if data was available
**     0 if the timer expired or a signal occurred.
*/
int waitread(fd, time)
int fd, time;
{
  fd_set readbits, other;
  struct timeval timer;
  int ret;
  timerclear(&timer);
  timer.tv_sec = time;
  FD_ZERO(&readbits);
  FD_ZERO(&other);
  FD_SET(fd, &readbits);
  ret = select(fd+1, &readbits, &other,
               &other, &timer);
  if (FD_ISSET(fd, &readbits))
  return 1;
  return 0;
}
```

```
/* ---------------- err.c ------------------- */

void syserr(msg)

/* print system call error message and terminate */

char *msg;
{

    extern int errno,sys_nerr;
    extern char *sys_errlist[];
    fprintf(stderr,"ERROR: %s (%d",msg,errno);

    if (errno > 0 && errno < sys_nerr)
        fprintf(stderr,";%s)\n",sys_errlist[errno]);
    else
        fprintf(stderr,")\n");
    exit(1);

}
```

3.2 Advanced Client/Server UNIX Network Programming in the TCP/IP UNIX and Internet Domains

by

Ted Mims

Objective: The purpose of this exercise is to give students experience in writing advanced network programming applications for the client/server model.

Brief Description: This module is an advanced programming assignment that requires students to implement a simple database server with one server and three clients. It requires the students to implement the server as a multiplexer that can accept requests from any of the three clients. These laboratory exercises have been utilized by students in an advanced course in UNIX network programming. The students' anxiety level was reduced by allowing them to work through easy message-passing exercises and providing them with simple examples from which to work.

Audience: Students who are learning the advanced concepts in UNIX network programming related to the client/server model for processes communicating over a network. They should have a working knowledge of C and UNIX, and the system calls socket, bind, listen, accept, connect, select, read, write and close for using sockets.

Equipment: A UNIX system that will support the TCP/IP UNIX and Internet domains, most graphics workstations including those by HP, SUN, Silicon Graphics, NeXT, and DEC. PCs running the Linux operating system also provide an appropriate platform.

Duration: Three weeks.

PROCEDURE:

LABORATORY EXERCISE I

This laboratory exercise will be implemented in the TCP/IP UNIX domain. Write a server program that allows three client processes to communicate with each other simulating a star network using sockets. The server program should establish socket connections with each of the three clients. The clients will have a menu that allows the user to 1) choose which of the other clients they wish to send a message to, 2) print the messages currently held in the messages file for this client, 3) delete the messages currently held in the messages file for this client, and 4) exit the program.

Once the user chooses the other client to which the message is to be sent, he/she will be prompted for a message that can have a maximum size of 40 characters. When the user enters a carriage return or reaches the 40 character limit, the message will be transmitted to the destination client via the server. The IDs of the transmitting and destination clients will be attached to the message. After the message is transmitted, the transmitting client will return to the menu. The server will display the message on its screen and pass the message to the appropriate client. The receiving client will write the message to its messages file. When the user selects print messages from the menu, the client will print all messages that are currently in the file. When the user selects remove messages, the client will delete all messages currently held in the messages file for that client. When the user selects exit from the menu, that node will be removed from the network (the socket connection to the server will be closed). When all clients have exited, the server will exit.

Lab Report:

a. Write a fully documented source listing of the sever and three client programs. Be sure to explain all sections that involve complicated system calls.

b. Indicate sample output from the three clients and the server.

LABORATORY EXERCISE 2

Implement exercise 1 to run in the Internet domain, using different platforms if available.

Lab Report:

a. Write a fully documented source listing of the sever and three client programs. Be sure to explain all sections that involve complicated system calls.

b. Indicate sample output from the three clients and the server.

3.3 Creating an International Time Zone Server and Client with UNIX Sockets Programming

by

Ann Burroughs

Objective: To increase student understanding of client-server technology by creating a time-zone server, using UNIX sockets programming.

Brief Description: Students modify two C programs which use sockets for computer-to-computer communication. The server program responds to client requests by looking up a city in a table and sending back the International Time Zone. The client repeatedly prompts the user for the name of a city and presents that city to the server for a response, then relays the response to the user. The client software runs on a computer separate from the server software.

Audience: General, but students must have C/C++ programming experience.

Equipment: At least two networked UNIX workstations with C/C++ compilers, available sockets libraries and TCP/IP. This exercise can be done using one station, but its pedagogic power comes from using two separate stations, which can be separated by small or large geographical distances, just as real-world clients are separated from the servers they use.

Duration: One to two weeks if working independently; two to three hours if working under direct faculty supervision, depending on students' programming experience.

PROCEDURE:

It's OK to work on this project in teams of two persons. It's also perfectly acceptable to work alone.

There is a tutorial on sockets programming available at *www.ecst.csuchico.edu/ ~beej/guide/net*. This document, written by Beej (Brian Hall at California State University, Chico), is a lucid explanation of sockets which you might find useful.

Included in that tutorial are two sample programs for communicating between processes running on separate computers, assuming underlying Internet protocols TCP/IP. These programs are given below. Very little modification has been done to Beej's original code. You will need your own copies of these programs.

First, you'll probably want to change the port number. The client communicates with the server and vice versa by means of a particular port. The programs use port number 3333, but if everyone in the class uses that number, there is the potential for conflict. You might want to pick your own number. Use a number greater than 1024 and less than 65535. Whatever number you choose for the server, you should use also for the client.

Next, you'll need to compile the programs. The compilation line for the server is:

```
gcc inetserv.c -oinetserv -lsocket -lnsl
```

You need both libraries specified so that the linker can resolve all the external references which these programs use.

Third, invoke the server on a particular machine. It should display "listening." It will then block (wait) until a connection is received.

From another station, Telnet to your server. Suppose your server is running on *ws22*. From, for instance, station *ws23*, you would Telnet to your server with this command:

```
telnet ws22 <portnumber>
```

That is, if you chose port number 3333 for the server, the command would be:

```
telnet ws22 3333
```

You should see

```
Hello, Internet world!
Connection closed by foreign host.
```

print out on the client, and on the server machine you see

```
listening
accepted
server: got connection from 137.150.188.43
listening
```

You now know your server is working.

Leave the server running on your first machine, and on your second machine invoke your client: *inetclnt ws22*. You should see behavior on both sides identical to the previous example, except that the client side will not display the "Connection closed" message. You should be able to Telnet and/or run the client multiple times from the second machine; the server is in an infinite loop and responds to each instance of a connection request from a client.

You'll need to Ctrl-C out of the server. If you reinvoke the server right away, there will be a problem with the bind statement—probably because the server process opened some kernel resources by its use of socket() and bind() that were not cleaned up, so the port stays allocated to the (now terminated) process until some cleanup daemon cleans it up. If you wait a minute or two, the situation will be cleaned up and you can reuse your server.

There are two more program files you now need: *itzserv.c* and *cities.txt*. These are also given below.

The file *cities.txt* consists of several records. Each record has two items: a city name and an international time zone (ITZ). See the end of the exercise for a listing of this file.

Your goal is to upgrade the server so that it "serves" ITZ information upon request from the client. The client will get the name of a city from the interactive user and send that name to the server; the server will look that city up in its data base and return the associated ITZ to the client for display to the interactive user.

Some of the work has been done for you. The program *itzserv.c* has all the functionality of *inetserv.c*. In addition, it reads the file *cities.txt* and stores that information into two arrays, *city* and *itz*. You need only write a search on the *city* array to match with the city the client requests, and return either the associated ITZ or some sort of "not found" information. It's up to you to determine the convention for sending the "not found" information from the server to the client, but the client needs to display "City not found" when this situation occurs.

WHAT YOU'LL STILL NEED TO DO:

1. Change "Hello, Internet world!" to some message indicating that the server is waiting to be asked about a city.

2. Add a loop to the client asking the user to enter a city. If you're using C, you probably want to use scanf for this purpose; here's a C code snippet that might work:

   ```
   char cityname[20];
       . . .
       printf("Enter the name of the city:    ");
   scanf('%s', cityname);
   ```

   You'll have to decide how to instruct the user to terminate the loop when he/she is done using the program. Since the *scanf* statement expects a string, you could use an asterisk, for instance.

3. Add code inside this loop to send the city entered by the user to the server, in addition to getting the server response back and printing it out.

4. Add code outside this loop, after the loop is over, which sends information to the server that it is OK to close the connection. You decide the convention for this interaction—it can be anything as long as both client and server agree.

5. Add code to the server to:

   a. receive the name of the city from the client;

   b. look up the city in the "data base" (array *city*);

   c. return the associated ITZ or some sort of "not found" information;

   d. repeat these steps until told by the client to close the connection. Only then should the *close(new_sd)* instruction be executed.

You might want to delay putting in the loops until the client is successfully sending one city name to the server and getting back a correct ITZ.

Lab Report:

Turn in a listing of each of your final programs, and a listing of the client's execution results when the user enters this sequence of cities: Ferndale, London, Kyoto, Singapore, Trinidad, Eureka, Sacramento, Arcata and your end-of-data sentinel.

File listings follow:

inetclnt.c

```c
#include <stdio.h>
#include <stdlib.h>
#include <errno.h>
#include <string.h>
#include <netdb.h>
#include <sys/types.h>
#include <netinet/in.h>
#include <sys/socket.h>

#define PORT 3333

#define MAXDATASIZE 100

int main(int argc, char *argv[])
{
  int csd;/* socket descriptor for the client  */

  int numbytes, x;
  char buf[MAXDATASIZE];
  struct hostent *he;
  struct sockaddr_in their_addr;  /* connector's
    (client's) info */
  if (argc != 2) {
  printf ("usage: client hostname\n");
  exit(1);
  }

  if ((he = gethostbyname(argv[1])) == NULL) {
  perror("gethostbyname");
  exit(1);
  }

/* now the user has invoked the program correctly  */

  if ((csd = socket(AF_INET, SOCK_STREAM, 0)) == -1) {
  perror("socket");
  exit(1);
  }

/* we successfully got a socket descriptor  */
```

```
        their_addr.sin_family = AF_INET;
        their_addr.sin_port = htons(PORT);
        their_addr.sin_addr = *((struct in_addr *)he->h_addr);
        /*bzero(&(their_addr.sin_zero), 8);*/
        for (x = 0; x < 7; x++) their_addr.sin_zero[x] = '0';

        if (connect(csd, (struct sockaddr *)&their_addr,
                 sizeof(struct sockaddr)) == -1) {
          perror("connect");
          exit(1);
        }

        if ((numbytes=recv(csd, buf, MAXDATASIZE,0)) == -1) {
          perror("recv");
          exit(1);
        }

        buf[numbytes] = '\0';

        printf("Received: %s", buf);

        close(csd);

        return 0;

        }
```

inetserv.c

```
#include <stdio.h>
#include <stdlib.h>
#include <errno.h>
#include <string.h>
#include <sys/types.h>
#include <netinet/in.h>
#include <sys/socket.h>
#include <sys/wait.h>

#define MYPORT 3333  /* the port users will connect to */

#define BACKLOG 10   /* maximum pending connections    */

main()
{

int sd;/* socket sd to listen on          */
int new_sd;/* socket to communicate with      */

/*u_long connecting;
int dot1, dot2, dot3, dot4;*/
int x;

struct sockaddr_in my_addr;/* my address information*/
```

```
struct sockaddr_in their_addr; /* connector's address
info*/
int sin_size;



if ((sd = socket(AF_INET, SOCK_STREAM, 0)) == -1) {
  perror("socket");
  exit(1);
}

/* now we have a socket connection for listening */

my_addr.sin_family = AF_INET; /* host byte order */
my_addr.sin_port = htons(MYPORT);  /* short, network
byte order */
my_addr.sin_addr.s_addr = INADDR_ANY; /* auto-fill with
my IP */

/*bzero(&(my_addr.sin_zero), 8); */  /* zero the rest of
the struct */

for (x = 0; x < 7; x++) my_addr.sin_zero[x] = '0';



if (bind(sd, (struct sockaddr *)&my_addr, sizeof(struct
sockaddr))
      == -1) {
    perror("bind");
    exit(1);
}

if (listen(sd, BACKLOG) == -1) {
  perror("listen");
  exit(1);
}

/* and our socket is now successfully listening  */

while(1) {
  sin_size = sizeof(struct sockaddr_in);
printf("listening\n");
  if ((new_sd = accept(sd, (struct sockaddr
*)&their_addr,
    &sin_size)) == -1) {
    perror("accept");
    continue;
  }
printf("accepted\n");

/* at this point we have received and accepted a connec-
tion request
*/
```

```
        printf("server: got connection from %s\n",
                    inet_ntoa(their_addr.sin_addr));

    /* at this point, if we were expecting more connections,
        we would fork a child process to handle the interaction,
        but we're not going to be that complicated!
    */

    if (send(new_sd, "Hello, Internet world!\n", 23,0) == -
1)
        perror("send");

    /* we're sending a message back to the connecting pro-
cess */

    close(new_sd);

    }   /* end while */

    }
```

itzserv.c

```
#include <stdio.h>
#include <stdlib.h>
#include <errno.h>
#include <string.h>
#include <sys/types.h>
#include <netinet/in.h>
#include <sys/socket.h>
#include <sys/wait.h>

#define MYPORT 3333   /* the port users will connect to */

#define BACKLOG 10   /* maximum pending connections    */

char *city[100];      /* an array of character pointers */
int itz[100];         /* an array of integers           */
int i;                /* i holds size of city array     */

/* This function fills the arrays city and itz with value
*/
/* the file "cities.txt". When the server gets a request
*/
/* to return the international time zone of a particular
*/
/* city, it can search through the city array for a match
*/
/* and return the corresponding location in the itz ar-
ray */

void fill_array()  {
```

```c
        char cityin[20];
        int itzin;
        int j;
        FILE *fp;
        fp = fopen("cities.txt", "r");
        while (fscanf(fp, "%s %d", cityin, &itzin) > 0) {
            city[i] = (char *) malloc(strlen(cityin) + 1);
            strcpy(city[i], cityin);
            itz[i] = itzin;
            i++;
        }
    /* You can pull this for loop out if you like. All
       it does is print out the contents of the city and
       its arrays. But you might want it for debugging
       purposes.
    */
     for (j = 0; j < i; j++)
         printf(" %s   %d \n", city[j], itz[j]);
}

main()
{

int sd;/* socket sd to listen on            */
int new_sd;/* socket to communicate with       */

/*u_long connecting;
int dot1, dot2, dot3, dot4;*/
int x;

struct sockaddr_in my_addr;/* my address information*/
struct sockaddr_in their_addr; /* connector's address
info*/
int sin_size;

fill_array();

/* now the city and itz arrays have values */

if ((sd = socket(AF_INET, SOCK_STREAM, 0)) == -1) {
  perror("socket");
  exit(1);
}

/* now we have a socket connection for listening */

my_addr.sin_family = AF_INET; /* host byte order */
my_addr.sin_port = htons(MYPORT);  /* short, network
byte order */
my_addr.sin_addr.s_addr = INADDR_ANY; /* auto-fill with
my IP */
```

```
    /*bzero(&(my_addr.sin_zero), 8); */  /* zero the rest of
    the struct */

    for (x = 0; x < 7; x++) my_addr.sin_zero[x] = '0';


    if (bind(sd, (struct sockaddr *)&my_addr, sizeof(struct
    sockaddr))
         == -1) {
      perror("bind");
      exit(1);
    }

    if (listen(sd, BACKLOG) == -1) {
      perror("listen");
      exit(1);
    }

    /* and our socket is now successfully listening  */

    while(1) {
      sin_size = sizeof(struct sockaddr_in);
    printf("listening\n");
      if ((new_sd = accept(sd, (struct sockaddr
    *)&their_addr,
        &sin_size)) == -1) {
        perror("accept");
        continue;
      }
    printf("accepted\n");

    /*  at this point we have received and accepted a
        connection request
    */

    printf("server: got connection from %s\n",
               inet_ntoa(their_addr.sin_addr));

    /* at this point, if we were expecting more connections,
       we would fork a child process to handle the interaction
    */

    if (send(new_sd, "Hello, Internet world!\n", 23,0) == -
    1)
        perror("send");

    /* we're sending a message back to the connecting pro-
    cess */

    close(new_sd);

    }  /* end while */

    }
```

cities.txt

```
Arcata 4
Eureka 4
Fortuna 4
Ferndale 4
Tucson 5
London 12
Sydney 22
Kyoto 21
Honolulu 2
Boston 7
Singapore 18
```

3.4 Airlines Reservation System

by

William Teter

Objective: Implement a client/server database in a UNIX environment programming in C.

Brief Description: This is a term project done by groups of students, three to a group. Students will meet weekly with the professor for updates on progress and help with design issues and coding problems. Students will be expected to write precise specifications for modules in the system and test them.

Audience: Students should understand the UNIX operating system, particularly locks, semaphores, pipes and sockets. In addition to network communication between processes there are issues of mutual exclusion involved which students should appreciate before they begin to design.

Equipment: A UNIX- or Linux-based network of computers.

Duration: One term or four weeks.

PROCEDURE:

A central computer holds the database for airlines reservations for Adirondack Air which runs four flights numbered 1 through 4. The plane capacities for these flights are 5, 2, 10 and 10, respectively. Travel agents from all over the world can access the reservation system by running a local application which calls up the central computer and runs an interactive session that supports the following commands:

Format of command

Query for number of seats available on flight x: Q x

Reserve seats i, j, etc. under name nm: R i j . . nm

Cancel seats for flight x under name n: C x n

The query command will first display the seat numbers of all the available seats on flight x if there are any. If none are available, the query ends with the message "none available." Otherwise, the travel agent may book any number of those seats for a name (say Jones) with the command R 1 6 2 9 Jones. Here 1 6 2 9 is the list of seats that are to be reserved for Jones. You should check that the requested seats are in the list of available seats. Any number of agents may access the reservation system concurrently. You will need to lock the flight record for the duration of this transaction so no other agent can take an available seat in the interim. If there is already a lock on the data, the server should send an explanatory message to the travel agent, because the agent will have to wait. If the travel agent responds with a C (cancel), terminate the query without allocating any seats.

Cancel should make available all seats under the given name on the specified flight, and then display the current number of seats now available.

On the server's monitor, display the current state of the database in real time. Indicate which seats are reserved and by whom. As soon as a change occurs, the screen should be updated. On the same screen show which clients are currently active.

The system should be robust in the sense that any erroneous command elicits a reasonable error message. Communication over the network will use sockets. The database will be in one file. The data on the file will be locked at the record level by the UNIX lock system call. The server will fork a child to handle each new interactive session from a travel agent. Use pipes to communicate between server and children.

Lab Report:

You must write the specifications for each of the programs involved in the system, including the format for data communicated over pipes and sockets.

3.5 Dining Philosophers

by

Daisy F. Sang

Objective: to experience Inter-Process Communication (IPC) and to experience client/server model by implementing the Dining Philosophers problem.

Brief Description: The Dining Philosophers problem is stated as follows: Five philosophers are seated around a circular table. Each philosopher has a plate of especially slippery spaghetti. The spaghetti is so slippery that a philosopher needs two forks to eat it. Between each plate is a fork. The life of a philosopher consists of alternate periods of eating and thinking. When a philosopher gets hungry, he/she tries to acquire his/her forks, eats for a while, then puts down the forks and continues to think.

Audience: A course on Computer Networking and Distributed Computing.

Equipment: Workstations running UNIX.

Duration: Two weeks.

PROCEDURE:

Your program should use the system calls provided by the UNIX operating system and be able to:

1. create child processes,

2. initiate a socket for each process,

3. use the socket to do IPC,

4. avoid a possible deadlock, and

5. close and unlink the socket.

Five child processes are to be created for five philosophers. The philosophers change their states among "thinking," "waiting" (for forks), and "eating," until all philosophers fulfill their eating requirements (60 seconds total eating time). The parent process (the server) accepts requests for granting and releasing forks from the child processes.

The hints to satisfy the above criteria are as follows.

1. The fork() system call can be used to create a child process.

2. The datagram (for connectionless service) type of socket should be initiated for each process, including the parent and child processes.

3. The sendto() and recvfrom() system calls can be used to send and receive messages respectively.

4. "Hold and wait" is restricted to break all possible deadlocks; i.e., a philosopher has to give up the fork (if he is currently holding one) if his request for another fork is rejected by the server.

5. The close() and unlink() system calls are used to remove the socket.

Lab Report:

Print the status of each philosopher whenever there is a change in the status (see the sample output on next page).

Your project will be graded based on correctness, generality, and efficiency.

SAMPLE OUTPUT:

Current time	philo #0	philo #1	philo #2	philo #3	philo #4
Sep 24 14:13:55	thinking	thinking	thinking	thinking	thinking
Sep 24 14:13:56	....	....	waiting	....	....
Sep 24 14:13:56	....	....	eating	....	....
Sep 24 14:13:58	....	....	....	waiting	....
Sep 24 14:14:01	....	....	....	....	waiting
Sep 24 14:14:01	....	....	....	....	eating
Sep 24 14:14:07	waiting	....	....	....	....
Sep 24 14:14:09	....	waiting	....	....	....
Sep 24 14:14:09	....	....	....	....	....
Sep 24 14:14:11	....	....	....	....	thinking
Sep 24 14:14:11	eating	....	....	....	....
Sep 24 14:14:12	....	....	....	....	....
Sep 24 14:14:12	....	....	thinking	....	....
Sep 24 14:14:12	....	....	....	eating	....
Sep 24 14:14:14	....	....	....	....	waiting
Sep 24 14:14:16	....	....	waiting	....	....

Sep 24 14:15:48	....	....	finished	....	....

Sep 24 14:15:48		....		....		....		eating		....
Sep 24 14:15:53		....		waiting		....		....		....
Sep 24 14:15:53		....		eating		....		....		....
Sep 24 14:15:53		waiting		....		....		....		....

Until all five philosophers finish eating.

3.6 Dining Philosophers II

by

Daisy F. Sang

Objective: To experience the Inter-Process Communication (IPC) and distributed processing by implementing the Dining Philosophers problem without using shared memory.

Brief Description: The Dining Philosophers problem is stated as follows: Five philosophers are seated around a circular table. Each philosopher has a plate of especially slippery spaghetti. The spaghetti is so slippery that a philosopher needs two forks to eat it. Between each plate is a fork. The life of a philosopher consists of alternate periods of eating and thinking. When a philosopher gets hungry, he/she tries to acquire his/her forks, eats for a while, then puts down the forks and continues to think.

Audience: A course on Computer Networking and Distributed Computing.

Equipment: Workstations running UNIX.

Duration: Two weeks.

PROCEDURE:

PROJECT DESCRIPTION:

Your program should be able to

1. create five child processes for philosophers, say Pi where 0 (i (4, and five child processes for forks, say Ci where 0 (i (4,

2. initiate a pair of sockets for each connection,

3. use the socket to do IPC,

4. avoid a possible deadlock, and

5. close and unlink the socket.

To satisfy the above criteria, you ought to do the following:

1. The fork() system call can be used to create a child process. The parent process should do nothing but create ten child processes. The requests for grant-

ing and releasing forks should be done by each child process Pi through the communication with the two corresponding fork processes.

2. The connection-oriented type of sockets should be initiated for each connection between Pi and Ci, and between Pi and $C_{(i+4) \bmod 5}$. The datagram type of sockets should be initiated for each connection between the parent and child processes, including both Pi and Ci, for all i.

3. The write() and read() system calls can be used to send and receive messages respectively in the connection-oriented communication.

4. "Hold and wait" is restricted to break all possible deadlocks; i.e., a philosopher has to give up the fork (if he/she is currently holding one) if his/her request for another fork is rejected by the server.

5. The close() and unlink() system calls are used to remove the socket.

Five child processes are to be created for five philosophers. The philosophers change their states among "thinking," "waiting" (for forks), and "eating," until all philosophers fulfill their eating requirements (60 seconds total eating time).

Lab Report:

Print the status of each philosopher whenever there is a change on the status (see sample output of the previous project).

Your project will be graded based on correctness, generality, and efficiency.

3.7 Three-Way Talk: An Extension to UNIX Two-Way Talk Laboratory

by

Lawrence J. Osborne

Objective: To introduce students to Internet protocols

Brief Description: Talk is a visual form of write. Using sockets, a two-way connection is set up between two people. With the aid of cursors, the screen is split into two windows, and each user's text is added to the window, one character at a time. Extend this program so that one user can talk to two other users instead of one. Usually, talk is a server which listens at UDP port 517. The actual conversation takes place on a TCP connection that is established by negotiation. The Internet services daemon, inedt, handles the execution of talkd.

Audience: Students who understand pipes, sockets and other UNIX system calls.

Equipment: UNIX

Duration: Four to five weeks.

PROCEDURE:

Your program needs to consider the following issues:

1. When two-way talk is in progress, one of the participants may want to initiate a second talk or may receive a talk request from another user.

2. A participant involved in a two-way talk should be able to escape from talking and issue another talk request.

3. When a second talk connection is established, the screen of the participant who issued the second talk request should be split into three windows.

4. To make three-way talk realistic, the screens of the other two participants must also be divided into three windows.

5. When one of the participants in a three-way talk hangs up, the remaining participants should be able to continue talking with their screens restored to two windows.

Lab Report:

Demonstrate your program to the instructor. Submit your code.

3.8 911 Dispatcher Laboratory

by

Lawrence J. Osborne

Objective: To introduce students to the ideas of object-oriented network programming, agents, and sockets or RPCs. One or more daemons must also be established.

Brief Description: This program will provide customer service by a 911 dispatcher. Emergency personnel can move from place to place at the order of the dispatcher. The set of types of emergencies and the distribution of police, firefighters, and paramedics needed to handle the emergencies can be as complex as the students want. Students should use an object-oriented model to analyze, design and test the code.

Audience: Students who are familiar with C++ or Java programming, sockets and some understanding of TCP and UDP.

Equipment: C++ and UNIX.

Duration: Four to five weeks.

PROCEDURE:

The 911 dispatcher will have a database of fire, police and ambulance crews that can respond to emergencies at remote sites.

1. When an emergency call is received, the dispatcher evaluates it and requisitions personnel from the database.

2. If insufficient personnel are available, the dispatcher will accept only the available people and, using TCP, transmit them to the customer location.

3. When people have completed their emergency function, they are then returned to the dispatcher's available database by the dispatcher.

4. The database management system consists of three singly linked lists and a pointer to one of the linked lists. Each entity houses a specific occupation: Police Officer, Firefighter, or Paramedic.

5. The program should be written in C++ and network objects including agents. After an emergency is handled remotely, the remote host decides whether to retain some of the emergency personnel for longer than usual if the situation

warrants it. Students are encouraged to use an Object Request Broker architecture so that the clients do not have to know where the dispatcher is located. They can do other things while the Broker takes care of the migration of police, firefighters and paramedics to the client host.

6. If you are a good Java programmer, you might try to implement mobile agents that can send themselves (i.e., both code and data from an interrupted thread) from one site to another, simulating human behavior.

Lab Report:

Demonstrate your program to the instructor. Submit your code.

3.9 Network Programming with Sockets

by

Samir and Ahlam Tannouri

Objective: To implement client/server communication using Java.

Brief Description: In this program, the students will write a small Java program that will implement a network communication between client and server classes.

Audience: Students with knowledge of Java and Networking protocols.

Equipment: UNIX and Java.

Duration: Four hours.

PROCEDURE:

Write two classes in Java to implement a network communication between a client and a server using sockets.

To help you do this lab, here are some explanations about how the client/server systems work with socket technology:

NETWORK CLIENT:

The network client uses an address to ask for a connection to a remote computer or printer on the network (usually it asks for a service from a server). After it gets serviced, it disconnects from the network.

NETWORK SERVER:

The network server listens to the network and waits to receive a request from a client. If one is received without conflict with others, the server services that request and closes the connection.

DOMAIN ADDRESS:

For each computer or device connected to a network, there is a unique address to identify that device to the network. On the Internet, a TCP/IP protocol is used. The IP address is four bytes separated by dots (130.85.1.5), and each byte is an integer providing specific information. The domain name of the form <gl.umbc.edu> is converted by a Domain Name Service (DNS) to an IP address.

PORT NUMBER:

For large companies, multihomed[1] servers use numbered ports to identify the various computers providing the different services of the same server.

A port number is a 16-bit integer that is added to the domain address to provide a unique host reference. When a single domain name is associated with several IP addresses, each specified by its port number, we must provide both the domain name and the port number.

SOCKETS:

Originated by UNIX and gaining popularity, sockets have been adopted by Sun as the principal tool for data communication in Java.

The <java.net> package provides a set of classes and methods that make network programming an easy task.

Lab Report:

Hints:

To reduce the programming code to a minimum, just call a server that replicates back your request (ECHO) without any additional work.

1. Write the classes for the client and the server.

2. Write very simple test programs to test your classes.

Here are some classes and methods for use in writing classes for this lab:

	(class)	(method)
<java.net>		
	Socket	getInputStream() getOutputStream() close()
	ServerSocket	accept()
<java.io>		
	DataInputStream	read()
	DataOutputStream	write()

---

[1] There might be multiple IP addresses associated with a given host name.

3.10 Inter-Applet Communication

by
Frances S. Grodzinsky
and
Sherman Corning

Objective: To allow applets on the same Web page to communicate with each other.

Brief Description: In order for applets to communicate with each other, they must be on the same Web page. Students will design two applets, each with two buttons. One updates the applet in which it resides, the second updates the other applet.

Audience: Students with an understanding of Networking and Java.

Equipment: Java and Web page posting capabilities.

Duration: Two weeks.

PROCEDURE:

1. Students will write two applets, Net1 and Net2.

2. Each applet should be designed with two buttons apiece. Button one will update the applet in which the button resides; button two will update the other applet.

3. Both applets should reside on the same Web page.

4. Both applet source files must be typed in and saved before compilation of either one.

5. The first applet, Net1, should contain a handlEvent() method.

6. Using the methods, getApplet() from the AppletContext class and the getAppletContext() from the Applet class, create an interface in which to call the methods of the Net2class and apply it to the applet itself. This allows you to control the applet by calling it with the name of the variable and the name in the applet tag assigned to it. In this case, "net2applet" controls the applet from within Net1.

7. When calling handleEvent(), make sure that you reference the particular event that interests you. For example,

```
//from Net1applet        return net2applet.han-
dleEvent(evt);
 //from Net2applet

  ...
else if ("Update Net2".equals(evt.arg))
 {str = "You updated me from Net 1"; repaint(); return
true }
```

8. Submit your Web address so the professor can run the inter-applet communication.

PART 4

NETWORK AND PERFORMANCE EXPERIMENTS

4.1 A Lan Protocol Analyzer: "LANdecoder"

by

Essaid Bouktache

Objective: The objective of this lab is to be exposed to LAN protocol analyzer software from Triticom, Inc., the "LANdecoder."

Brief Description: The analyzer can be used to capture and decode Ethernet, Token-Ring, ArcNet frames and other layers of the OSI model. The analyzer, which comes in a single diskette, is run from any workstation attached to a network, and runs without loading the network drivers. This means you don't need to log in to the network. In fact, the software might not run if you do. The analyzer can capture frames exchanged between workstations that are logged in to the network. Your objective in this lab is to capture Ethernet frames and do a thorough analysis of the different fields within each frame using the provided protocol analyzer.

Audience: Undergraduate students with a knowledge of LAN frame formats and some knowledge of the lower four layers of the OSI networking architecture model.

Equipment: The diskette containing the "LANdecoder" from Triticom (Eden Prairie, MN), 80286 PC or above for the station running the analyzer, network adapter card for the station running the analyzer (Ethernet, Token Ring, or ARC-NET), and networked PCs (the software supports any adapter that works with Novell's Open Data Link Interface, or ODI).

Duration: Three hours.

PROCEDURE:

1. First, in order to use the LAN analyzer, you need to know the *Port* and *Interrupt* numbers of your workstation. Therefore, log in as usual and type USER-LIST/A to obtain these two parameters.

2. Log out and reboot your PC to get rid of the network drivers that are loaded in memory.

3. Change to the directory LANDECOD.

4. If you have an Eagle card, type:

```
C:\LANDECOD> LDE NE2000 /PXXX /IX <Enter>
```

PXXX being the port # and IX being the interrupt number you noted in step 1).

5. If you have an Intel card, type:

```
C:\LANDECOD> LDE INTELEXP /PXXX /IX <Enter>
```

PXXX being the port number and IX being the interrupt number you noted in step 1).

6. In the next screen that appears, notice all the different protocols that the LAN analyzer can decode.

7. In the "Adapter Configuration" window, write down the adapter MAC address, which is the physical address of the network interface card (48 bits). (That information was also available in step 1.)

8. Select "Capture Traffic." At this point, at least one workstation should be logged in to the network.

9. The first frame captured comes from the server and carries a broadcast address to all stations. Notice the direction of transmission at the top of the screen (from A to B, or from B to A.)

10. At the server console, type SEND 'HI' <Enter> to broadcast this message. Notice that all stations running the analyzer will have the number of frames sent by the server updated.

11. Back at the stations, press F2 to toggle between the station name at the top of the screen and the address in hexadecimal notation (six bytes, or 48 bits).

12. After you have captured a few frames, press <Esc>.

13. From the main menu, select "Decode Frames."

14. Press F2 so that the destination and source addresses appear in hexadecimal.

15. Use the up/down arrows to select a frame; then press <Enter>.

16. When the new screen appears, press <Page Up> a few times to go to the top of the window.

17. The decoding of the frame starts at the MAC (Medium Access Layer) sublayer. Notice that in the "Hexadecimal" window, the bytes that correspond to the header you select are highlighted.

18. The detailed information is displayed for the following four different sublayers:

   a. MAC (Medium Access Control), this is the lower part of the Data Link Layer

   b. DLC (Data Link Control), this is the upper part of the Data Link Layer

   c. IPX (Internetwork Packet Exchange)

   d. NCP (NetWare Core Protocol)

19. Using the down arrow, scroll down one line at a time, and for each line in the top window, you should identify and write down the bytes that are highlighted in the "Hexadecimal" window. For example, when you highlight the des-

tination address in the Ethernet frame, you should see six bytes highlighted in hexadecimal.

20. Identify the **two bytes** which indicate the length of the data field. Convert that to decimal in order to find out if the frame needs padding bytes. For example, if that number is 44 bytes, you should expect to see two bytes in the padding field to make **the minimum of 46** that is required in the data portion. Verify this by counting the number of bytes which follow the length field up to but not including the CRC, which is four bytes.

21. Continue down to the last layer which is the NCP (NetWare Core Protocol).

22. The **IPX** sublayer: Identify every field of this sublayer as you move down with the arrow key, and write down how many bytes are taken by each field. Pay particular attention to the destination host address, which must be the same as the address shown at the top of the screen.

23. The **NCP** (NetWare Core Protocol) sublayer: This is the higher layer of the Novell NetWare stack which plays the role of the Session Layer in the OSI model. Since one of the responsibilities of this layer is to establish a connection, you should pay attention to the presence of a **Sequence #** and a **Connection #**.

24. After you are done surfing the different fields, press <Esc> to go back to the main menu and select "Manage Names." Use the arrow key to select a frame by its hexadecimal address; then press <Enter>. Press <Enter> again and type a name for that station. If the server address is also there, just type SERVER1 for the name. For the other stations, type S1, S2, S3, etc., or use any other name that could be appropriate.

25. Once the names are entered, press <Esc> to backup to the main menu and select "Capture Frames." When the window which shows the captured frames appears, press F2 to toggle between the hexadecimal and the true names of all stations.

26. Play with the other keys displayed at the bottom of the screen to learn about other things you can do with this software package.

Preamble	Dest. Addr.	Source Addr.	Data Length	Data	PAD	CRC
8 Bytes	2 or 6	2 or 6	2	0-1500	?	4

Figure 1 IEEE 802.3 Frame Format.

Preamble	Dest. Addr.	Source Addr.	Frame Type	Data	CRC
8 Bytes	6	6	2	46-1500	4

Figure 2 Ethernet Frame Format.

SD	AC	FC	DA	SA	DATA	CRC	ED	FS
1	1	1	2 or 6	2 or 6		4	1	1

Figure 3 Token Ring (IEEE 802.5) Frame Format.

HIGHER-LEVEL PROTOCOLS

The following information could be useful in decoding the higher-level protocols with "LANdecoder."

Novell NetWare communications services offer two types of PC-to-PC or PC-to-Server communication protocols:

a. A Datagram Protocol: IPX (Internerwork Packet Exchange)

b. A Connection-Oriented Protocol: SPX (Sequenced Packet Exchange)

1. IPX: A DATAGRAM SERVICE

IPX is a connectionless protocol supported by Novell NetWare which is based on datagrams. It performs addressing, routing, and switching to deliver a packet to its destination. NetWare Shell/Redirector software uses IPX to send and receive packets to and from the file server. Novell claims that IPX packets are correctly received about 95% of the time. IPX corresponds to the Network Layer in the OSI model.

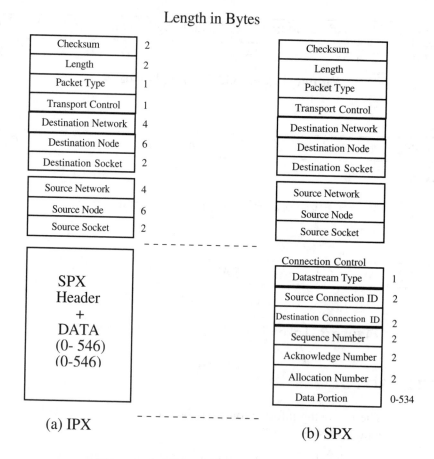

Length in Bytes

(a) IPX   (b) SPX

Figure 4 IPX and SPX Packet Format.

2. SPX: A CONNECTION-ORIENTED SERVICE

SPX is a connection-oriented protocol, or session-level protocol. Before data can be exchanged, a connection must be established between the sender and the receiver. SPX guarantees delivery as well as the order of arrival of packets. SPX operates one layer above IPX, at the Transport Layer. It also has some characteristics of the Session Layer.

IPX is included in Novell NetWare, but you may or may not have SPX, depending on your version of NetWare.

4.2 The Commkit Wide Area Network Emulator

by

Essaid Bouktache

Objective: The objective of the lab is to explore a few features of a network emulator software called Commkit, which comes in a single diskette and must be loaded in all PCs involved in the experiment. This software can emulate LANs (Ethernet, Token Ring), WANs (Wide Area Networks), Bridges, and various other aspects of networking protocols.

Brief Description: In this lab, we will emulate the X.25 connection-oriented packet-switching protocol. We will experiment the principles of the Stop-and-Wait protocol, Virtual Circuits, Call Request packets, Information Frames, Supervisory Frames, etc.

Audience: Undergraduate students with a minimum knowledge of the X.25 packet-switched public network.

Equipment: A diskette containing Commkit, a minimum of three PCs per station, with two serial ports per PC, and null-modem cables attached to the serial ports.

Duration: Three Hours.

SET-UP:

THE COMMKIT[1] SOFTWARE

The Commkit software is supplied in a 3.5" diskette and must be installed on all the computers that will be involved in the experiment. If the software is already installed, change to the subdirectory "COMMKIT." If the package is not installed, insert the diskette in a floppy drive and type "INSTALL C:". The software will create a subdirectory called "COMMKIT," where all its files will be stored.

This package contains networking routines like Stop-and-Wait, Virtual Circuits, CRC generation, etc., and has a line analyzer module which will display the contents of frames which are exchanged in a PC-to-PC communication. It can also

---

[1] Commkit Software is a component of *Introduction to Data Communications: A Practical Approach,* by Larry Hughes (1997), Sudbury, MA: Jones and Bartlett Publishers, Inc.

emulate the Bus topology (Ethernet), the Token-Passing network (Token Ring), and internetworking (Bridges.) The line analyzer runs in one of the PCs, which is usually in the middle.

CONNECTING THE COMPUTERS

Three computers must be connected to each other by the supplied NULL-MODEM cables, as shown in Figure 1 below. Port 1 of one computer must be connected to Port 2 of the other. The computer in the middle will run the Line Analyzer software.

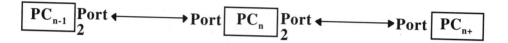

Figure 1 Ordering of Ports in the PC-to-PC Connections.

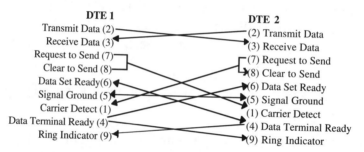

Figure 2 A Null-Modem Cable (9- or 25-pin connectors).

PROCEDURE:

THE "COMMKIT" LINE ANALYZER

The line analyzer, which runs in the middle computer in Figure 1, is a C program supplied in file "analyzer. c" which grabs data sent by one of the computers and displays the contents of each frame. The algorithm implemented by this software does the following:

a. Reads a byte

b. Displays the byte

c. Forwards the byte to the other port

Running the Line Analyzer:

Before you run any software on the other computers, you must first start the Line Analyzer on the middle computer, marked PC_n in Figure 1. The executable file of the Line Analyzer is **"analyser. exe"**.

To start the analyzer, change to subdirectory "COMMKIT" and type:

```
C:\COMMKIT>analyser LineSpeed <Enter>
```

where "LineSpeed" is the baud rate, which can be 50, 300, 1200, 2400, 4800, or 9600. For example:

```
C:\COMMKIT>analyser 9600 <Enter>.
   -Type Ctrl-S to stop the line analyzer.
   -Type Ctrl-Q to turn the line analyzer back ON.
   -Type Ctrl-C to exit the analyzer.
```

THE "COMMKIT" STOP-AND-WAIT PROTOCOL

The executable file of the Commkit Stop-and-Wait protocol is "**s&wex.exe**".

1. **Starting and Stopping the Protocol:**

   - To start the Stop-and-Wait protocol type the following *at the receiving computer first*: C:\COMMKIT>**s&wex** *LineSpeed PortNumber* **R** <Enter>, where "PortNumber" is the serial port number where the cable is connected. "R," which must be in *uppercase*, indicates "Receiver." Example: C:\COMMKIT>**s&wex 9600 2 R** <Enter>, to receive from serial port 2 at 9600 bps.

   - Start "s&wex" at the transmitting computer by typing:

     ```
     C:\COMMKIT>s&wex 9600 1 X <Enter>,
     ```

     to transmit through serial port 1 at 9600 bps.

   - To exit the program press **Ctrl-C**.

2. **Sending Messages:**

   Messages are forwarded by the transmitter if one of two things happens:

   a. 10 lines of text are typed (A line is either a carriage return or a full line on the screen.)

   b. Ctrl-Z is typed *after* <Enter> *is pressed* following any string of characters (less than 10 lines)

3. **Stop-and-Wait Exercise:**

   a. Make sure the line analyzer is running in the middle computer.

   b. Run the s&wex protocol at both end computers, according to step 1 above.

   c. From the transmitter (X), send a few messages and try to identify all the fields in the frames which are displayed on the line analyzer screen (the middle computer) as soon as you transmit a message. The message is also displayed at the receiver.

   d. Send a long message (10 lines), and notice how it is broken into packets.

   e. Try to determine the length of each packet.

   f. Identify the sequence numbers shown at the line analyzer P.

   g. On the line analyzer, the frame delimiters appear as (STX, for "Start of Text") and as a blank heart (ETX, for "End of Text"), while the acknowledgment appears as ♠ (ACK). The 2 bytes that follow the ETX are the CRC bytes.

h. Fill the screen (10 lines) at the transmitter with the same character and send it. *Explain the difference in the values of the CRC displayed on the analyzer.*

THE "COMMKIT" WIDE AREA NETWORK

The Commkit Wide Area Network software simulates the use of Virtual Circuits, such as those found in the packet-switched public network standard **X.25.** The executable file of the Commkit Wide Area Network is **"wanex.exe"**.

1. **Call Setup:**

Before data can be exchanged between the end computers, a path (Virtual Circuit) must exist between the two computers. The call setup is initiated by one of the end computers trying to create a **Virtual Circuit** with the computer at the other end. This is done with a **Call-Request** packet, which is shown in Figure 3. Both computers should send a Call-Request packet to each other for full-duplex transmission.

R	VC	DS	SR

Figure 3 Commkit Call-Request Packet.

Fields of the Call-Request Packet:

R   Indicates a Call-Request packet. *"R" Must be typed as uppercase.*

VCN   Virtual circuit number (a single character) assigned by the user. This number will distinguish between incoming calls and is not transmitted across the network.

DST   Destination address. This must be a single character.

SRC   Source node address, also a single character.

Call Setup Exercise:

a. Make sure the line analyzer is running in the middle computer.

b. At the computer of Figure 1 marked PC_{n+1}, type: C:\COMMKIT>**wanex 9600 s 3** <Enter>. Character "s" is the address of PC_{n+1}. The "3" is the window size. A blank screen will follow.

c. At the other computer, marked PC_{n-1}, type: C:\COMMKIT>**wanex 9600 e 3**<Enter>. Address of PC_{n-1} is "e," window size is 3.

d. At PC_{n+1}, type the Call-Request packet: **R4es** <Enter>. The VCN (Virtual Circuit Number) arbitrarily chosen is **4**. Later on, any incoming packet to this computer will have this number. The end computer, PC_{n-1}, should echo **R0es** in inverse video. The "0" will be the VCN for outgoing packets from PC_{n-1}.

Notes:

—When the Call-Request packet R4es was sent, the VCN "4" did not show on the line analyzer, since it was not transmitted.

—The first Call-Request packet must be initiated from the computer with an outgoing serial Port 1, as indicated in Figure 1.

e. At PC_{n-1}, type the Call-Request packet:

R6se <Enter>. Again, the VCN chosen is 6, and any incoming packet to this computer will contain this number. PC_{n+1} should echo **R1se** in inverse video. All outgoing packets from PC_{n+1} will have VCN #1.

The Virtual Circuits setup is summarized in Figure 4.

Figure 4 End-to-End Virtual Circuits.

f. Repeat the above and establish another virtual path using different virtual circuit numbers.

2. Data Transfer:

Once a Virtual Circuit has been established on both sides, data transfer can be initiated by either end computer. A message sent by one computer will be displayed in inverse video at the other computer. The line analyzer displays all fields within each packet. The format for the Commkit data packet is shown in Figure 5.

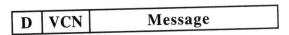

Figure 5 Commkit Data Packet.

Fields of the Data Packet:

D   Denotes a Data packet. *"D" must be typed as uppercase.*

VCN The Virtual Circuit number (a single character) assigned by the receiving computer in response to a Call-Request packet.

Message String of characters making up the message, followed by a carriage return (<Enter>).

Data Transfer Exercise:

a. This step must follow the Call-Setup exercise, so make sure the line analyzer is running in the middle computer (PC_n) and the virtual circuits have been established in both directions.

b. At PC_{n-1}, type:

D0 *How are you?* <Enter>.

The "**D**" indicates a data packet. The "**0**" is the virtual circuit for outgoing messages from this computer (shown as VCN#0 in Figure 4), as established by the Call-Request packet, followed by any message to be sent.

PC_{n+1} must display "**D4 How are you?**" in inverse video, where the "**4**" indicates the incoming virtual circuit number to this computer.

c. To verify transmission in both directions, go to PC_{n+1} and type:

D1 *I am fine.* <Enter>.

The "**1**" indicates the outgoing virtual circuit number from this computer, as indicated in Figure 4. PC_{n-1} must display "**D6 I am fine**" in inverse video, with "**6**" being the incoming VCN to this computer, again as shown in Figure 4.

d. Send several messages and try to identify the different fields within each packet. It would be easier to send a string of the same character.

3. Test Mode:

- The test mode allows the end computers to send packets to each other. The packets contain lowercase letters (from a to z).

- The test mode operates with a window size of **5** to avoid flooding the receive queue at each node.

- The test mode is entered by typing the uppercase letter **T** followed by the outgoing virtual circuit number.

a. At PC_{n-1}, type:

T0 <Enter>, since the outgoing VCN is 0 (see Figure 4).

The data packets should appear at PC_{n+1}. On the line analyzer, they can be recognized as having the uppercase "D" as the packet code.

b. To run the test mode simultaneously at both computers, go to PC_{n+1} and type:

T1<Enter>. Again, the outgoing VCN for this computer is **1**, as shown in Figure 4.

c. To stop the test mode, type:

S <Enter>. The letter must be *uppercase*.

4. Call Clearing:

Either one of the virtual circuits can be cleared by sending a Call-Clearing packet, whose format is shown in Figure 6. To clear the full-duplex communication link, each computer must send a Call-Clearing packet. A Call-Clearing packet is the uppercase **C** followed by the outgoing VCN.

Figure 6 Commkit Call-Clearing Packet.

a. To clear the path from PC_{n-1} to PC_{n+1}, go to PC_{n-1} and type **C0** <Enter>. This means you can no longer send messages on outgoing VCN#0 out of PC_{n-1}.

But you can still send packets from this computer on a different VCN, if you have created one or more.

b. Verify that you can still receive messages from PC_{n+1}, even though you cannot send messages out of PC_{n-1}. To do this, go to PC_{n+1} and send a few data packets.

c. Similarly, you can clear the other virtual circuit out of PC_{n+1} by typing **C1** <Enter> at PC_{n+1}.

d. Verify that both paths are cleared by trying to send data packets.

e. If you want to reestablish communications, you must build up the virtual circuits all over again, using Call-Request packets as was done before.

5. **Low-Level Testing:**

In this section, we will concentrate more on the types of frames being sent and the send and receive sequence numbers Ns and Nr, which are three-bit numbers used in the sliding window protocol. Commkit supports two types of frames: **Information and Supervisory.**

Supervisory frames are short and can easily be identified on the line analyzer screen. They contain a single character which represents the value of Nr (next frame expected). This character follows the STX symbol, followed by the two CRC bytes and, finally, the ETX symbol. Nr will appear on the line analyzer as one of the characters shown in Figure 7.

Nr	Internal Value	Displayed As
0	10000000	ç
1	10000001	Å
2	10000010	Ç
3	10000011	É
4	10000100	Ñ
5	10000101	Ö
6	10000110	Ü
7	10000111	ç

Figure 7 Representation of Nr in Commkit Supervisory Frames.

Information frames carry any data sent from one computer to the other. The character following the STX is the control field, which represents the values of both Ns and Nr, according to the partial table shown in Figure 8. For example, the symbol ♣ means Nr = 5 and Ns = 0. The third character is the packet code: **R** for Call-Request packets, **D** for Data, **C** for Call-Clearing (and **E** for Error). The rest are the data bytes. Prior to the ETX are the two CRC bytes. (If the CRC contains DLE or ETX, more bytes will appear, due to character stuffing.)

Nr \ Ns	0	1	2	3	4	5	6	7
0				0	@			p
1			!	1			Q	a
2								
3								
4			$					
5	♣	§	%					
6	♠							
7	♠							w

Figure 8 Representation of Nr and Ns in Commkit Information Frames.

Commkit Data Link Layer:

The frame format used in the Commkit link-to-link protocol is shown in Figure 9. All frames have the same format, beginning with STX (Start of Text) and ending with ETX (End of Text). The one-byte Control field indicates whether the frame is an I-frame or an S-frame. The field shown as "Information" is the Network Layer packet, which is shown in Figure 10. The CRC is a two-byte field represented by two characters on the line analyzer.

STX	Control (1)	Information (up to 128 Bytes)	CRC (2)	ETX

Figure 9 Commkit Data Link Layer Frame Format.

Commkit Network Layer:

The Commkit's network layer packet is shown in Figure 10. The packet code byte is either R (Call-Request), D (Data), C (Call-Clearing) or E (Error). The next byte is the virtual circuit number VCN used in the previous exercises. The third byte is either the called DTE's address used when the Call-Request packet is sent, or data. The fourth byte is either data or the calling DTE's address used in the Call-Request packet. The rest of the packet can be up to 126 bytes of data.

Field	Description
code	Packet code.
vcn	The virtual circuit number.
msg[0]	The called DTE's address (call request only), data, or an error code.
msg[1]	The calling DTE's address (call request only), otherwise data.
msg[2] through msg[126]	Up to 126 bytes of data.

Figure 10 Commkit Network Layer Packet Format.

6. **Low-Level Testing Exercise:**

    a. Start the line analyzer in the middle computer.

    b. Establish a full-duplex virtual circuit connection as was done in the previous exercises.

    c. Send nine messages (data packets) from one PC to the other. Watch the line analyzer screen every time you send a message, so that you know where the acknowledgment frames are displayed and where they start.

    d. After you send the nine messages, stop the analyzer by typing Ctrl-S. (Remember, Ctrl-Q will start it again.)

    e. Your objective is to recognize every frame sent and every field within a frame. Verify sequence numbers, control characters, CRC bytes, etc.

4.3 Experimenting with Message Delay, Collision Frequency, and Number of Simultaneous Users on a CSMA/CD Local Area Network

by

Ann Burroughs

Objective: Using a simulation tool, determine how the performance of a traditional Ethernet LAN degrades as more and more traffic is offered. As congestion begins to affect throughput, performance should degrade according to queuing-theory predictions, and packet delay times should begin to climb toward infinity.

Brief Description: Using COMNET III[1] to model a 25-station CSMA/CD LAN, we will allow first one station pair to communicate, then two station pairs, then three station pairs, and so on, until all station pairs are attempting to send/receive large files simultaneously. We will record and chart the utilization of the channel (the LAN), the average message delay, and the number of collisions, and we will make conclusions about the LAN performance under pressure.

Audience: General telecommunications/networking students.

Equipment: COMNET III running on workstations. Note that the newest academic release of COMNET III constrains the number of nodes to a maximum of 20. Older versions do not have this constraint. CACI has indicated a willingness to work with universities to overcome this artificial restriction; however, instructions will need to be revised according to the version of COMNET available to the students.

Duration: Two to three hours for building the model, running the simulations and capturing the data. Another one to two hours for constructing the lab write-up.

[1] Comnet III is a network simulation tool of CACI, La Jolla, California.

PROCEDURE:

We will be using COMNET III to model a typical Ethernet (CSMA/CD) LAN.

1. In COMNET, construct 25 processing nodes (24 workstations and one server). Construct one CSMA/CD link and associate all 25 processing nodes with that link. Move the workstation nodes so that about 12 of them are on the left side of the window and 12 are on the right. Name the 12 on the left A1, A2, ..., A12; name the 12 on the right B1, B2,..., B12. Name the other node SERVER. Save your model.

2. Add a message source to node A1. Edit the message source so it has these characteristics:

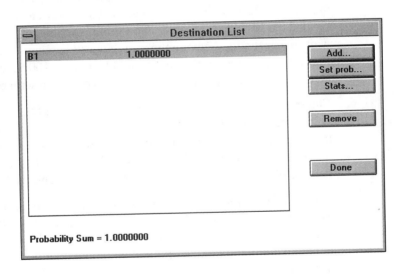

3. Use Edit Destination List to send all the message traffic to node B1:

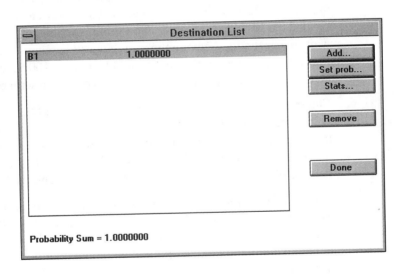

4. Set the simulation length to 30 seconds and turn on these reports: Collision Statistics (Links), Call Count (Links), Channel Utilization (Links) and Message Delay (Message and Response Sources).

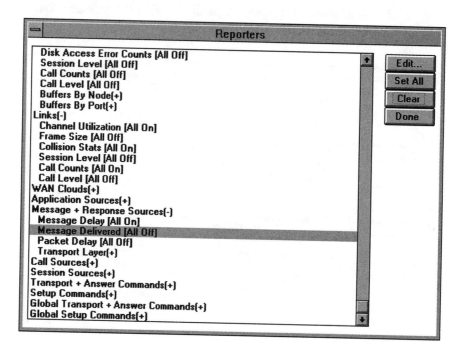

5. Run the simulation. Obviously, we are pushing much more traffic at the LAN than it can accommodate (8 Mb each 0.1 second translates to 80 Mbps, well beyond the 10-Mbps standard). You should see this reflected in the message-wait-time statistics, because the message wait times will grow exponentially. Further, the channel utilization should be almost 100%, and there should be no collisions. Check that your results are consistent with these predictions.

6. Change the message size to 10 K. Now we are presenting 800 kbps, well within the capabilities of the LAN. Run the simulation and determine that there are reasonable wait times for the messages and reasonable channel utilization (you should get about 8%, which is 800 K/10 M). Keep track of the number of collisions, the average message delay and the channel utilization.

7. Add an identical message source to node A2, except that it should connect exclusively to node B2. Run the simulation again. You should begin to see collisions, and the average message delay should be affected accordingly. Note the number of collisions, the average message delay and the channel utilization.

8. Keep adding message sources to Ax nodes, pairing them with the corresponding Bx node. Run the simulation each time you add a message source/node pairing. Be sure to gather the data as you go. When you are finished, you should have 12 sets of data. There should be a point at which you observe the delays beginning to increase dramatically.

9. Use Excel or some other graphing tool to graph the average message delay as the dependent variable and the number of sending nodes as the independent variable. Prepare another graph showing the collisions as the dependent variable and the number of sending nodes as the independent variable.

10. Modify the assumptions of the model by manipulating some combination of message size and interarrival times so that all message sources can be active without serious degradation of network performance. Keep all the message sources identical. What is the largest value for traffic presented at each node per second which can reasonably be handled by the network?

11. Obviously, a typical LAN will have much more random behavior in terms of traffic presented to the network. While temporary delays may occur, there should be sufficient bandwidth so that message queues do not lengthen infinitely. Change the message size to 5000B, the First Arrival to *none*, and the interarrival rate to the Exponential distribution with a mean of one. This means that a number will be randomly chosen from the Exponential distribution using a mean of one second. According to the documentation,

> This distribution is widely used to model arrival times of events which follow a Poisson pattern. Each sample chosen from the Exponential function specifies the time which will elapse before the next arrival. This is called the interarrival time. Samples have a high probability of being less than the mean. This implies that the distribution has a long tail and will occasionally provide a sample significantly higher than the mean. This behavior is very useful in modeling random arrival patterns.... The Exponential function is used to actually implement Poisson arrival patterns.[1]

You should know that Poisson arrival patterns are typically used in modeling random arrivals of traffic to computer networks. There has recently been some discussion in the theoretical literature about whether Poisson arrivals truly model the real world, but apparently it is the best approximation known.

Run the simulation and look at the results. Is the network taxed? Explain how you know.

12. Change the Exponential function mean to 10 seconds for each message source, and rerun the simulation. Is the network taxed now?

13. Add a Response Source to each of the B nodes. Make the message size the same as for the A nodes.

Run the simulation. Is the network taxed now? Explain how you know.

14. How many A-to-B pairs can this network accommodate with the present traffic pattern assumptions before it begins to degrade? You will probably have to add nodes to answer this question. You might want to add nodes in groups, rather than one at a time!

Lab Report:

Prepare a report which includes the raw data you collected to answer the questions above, as well as your graphs for step 9 and your answers to the questions raised in steps 10 through 14. Briefly discuss your results, comparing your expectations to the actual results and noting any anomalies or unexplained behaviors.

---

[1] *Comnet III Users Manual*, La Jolla, CA: CACI, 1995, p. 379.

4.4 Ethernet vs. Token Ring

by

Frances S. Grodzinsky

Objective: The goal of this lab is to monitor the characteristics of two of the most popular LAN architectures: Ethernet, which uses a bus topology, and CSMA/CD and Token Ring, which use a Ring topology and token passing as the access method.

Brief Description: Students will set up two identical simulations except for the LAN topology: one simulation will be set up as Ethernet and the other as Token Ring. Each network will consist of two LANs: a Customer LAN and a Distribution Center LAN that are connected by a Router. Also connected to the Router is the Sales Force Processing node, which is connected by a 56-kbps line. The Customer Service LAN will be connected to four nodes: the Customer Service group node, the Marketing group node, the Server 1 group node and the Router. The Distribution Center LAN will be connected to three nodes: the Order Distribution group node, the Server 2 group node and the router. Each node will execute at least one application. Simulations will be run with and without link failures and reports on performance generated.

Audience: Computer or information science students with a background in data communication or networking.

Equipment: Comnet III[1] simulation tool.

Duration: Two weeks.

[1] Comnet III is a product of CACI, La Jolla, California.

PROCEDURE:

Set up two simulations: an Ethernet and a Token Ring[1]. Each network will consist of two LANs: a Customer LAN and a Distribution Center LAN that are connected by a Router. Also connected to the Router is the Sales Force Processing node, which is connected by a 56-kbps line. The Customer Service LAN will be connected to four nodes: the Customer Service group node, the Marketing group node, the Server 1 group node and the Router. The Distribution Center LAN will be connect-

[1] This lab is based on a final project by James Barlow and Bonnie Schulte.

ed to three nodes: the Order Distribution group node, the Server 2 group node and the router. Each node will execute at least one application. All the nonserver nodes execute applications which execute transport message commands. These messages are sent to either server 1 or 2, depending upon their routing table. All messages with the prefix CDB are sent to server 1, and all messages with the prefix INV are sent to server 2.

1. Set up the simulation.

2. Before running the simulation, write a short paragraph about what you expect to happen. After you run the simulation, in your conclusions, compare your expectations to the actual results. Run your replications from one to 361 seconds.

3. **TEST 1**: Run the simulation **without link failures** first on Ethernet and then on Token Ring.

    - Generate reports on *packet delays for transport and answer commands* for the Ethernet and the Token Ring simulations.

    - Generate reports on *message delays for transport and answer commands* for the Ethernet and Token Ring simulations.

    - Generate a report on Random Access Link Performance on the Ethernet which is a Collision Statistics Report under Link.

4. **TEST 2**: Run the simulation **with a link failure** first on Ethernet and then on Token Ring.

    - Generate the same reports as above. Now you will have a report on both Ethernet and Token Ring, with and without failures.

5. **TEST 3**: Run **four traces** of the Order Processing application as it is simulated through the two networks when the Ethernet Network is completely operational, when the Ethernet's Distribution Center LAN is down, when the Token Ring Network is completely operational, and when the Distribution Token Ring and Router are down.

    The Order Processing application executes three commands: CDB REQUEST FOR DATA, INV REQUEST FOR DATA, and CDB PROCESS DATA. At the server, an application is executed that executes an answer command that returns a message to the original node. The application at server 1 (Customer Service Database) is set to answer all messages with the prefix CDB. The application at server 2 (Inventory Database) is set to answer all messages with the prefix INV. The CDB messages are sent over server 1 where the command CDB RETURN DATA is executed. The INV messages are sent to server 2 where the command INV RETURN DATA is executed.

    - Write a paragraph about what happened in each of these traces.

    - What were your general observations associated with the traces?

    - Include the trace screens for reference with your report. Using an editor cut and paste the appropriate references; otherwise, you will be printing out reams of paper for each trace.

Simulation setup and variables:

NODES

Customer Service
Type: Computer and Communications
Parameter: Parameter 1
Failure Time: EXP (10)
Repair Time: EXP (1.0)
Command:
    CDB Process Data
    (T) CDB Request Data
    INV Request Data

Order Distribution
Type: Computer and Communications
Parameter: Parameter 1
Failure Time: EXP (10)
Repair Time: EXP (1.0)
Command:
    CDB Process Data
    (T) CDB Request Data
    INV Request Data
    INV Process Data

Marketing
Type: Computer and Communications
Parameter: Parameter 1
Failure Time: EXP (10)
Repair Time: EXP (1.0)
Command:
    (T) CDB Request Data
Sales Force
Type: Computer and Communications
Parameter: Parameter 1
Failure Time: EXP (10)
Repair Time: EXP (1.0)
Command:
    INV Process Data

Server 1
Type: Computer and Communications
Parameter: Parameter 1
Failure Time: EXP (10)
Repair Time: EXP (1.0)
Command:
    (A) CDB Return Data

Server 2
Type: Computer and Communications
Parameter: Parameter 1
Failure Time: EXP (10)
Repair Time: EXP (1.0)
Command:
    INV Return Data

NODE PARAMETER

Parameter 1
Processing/cycle (mic): 1
Disk Storage (MB):   1200
Sector (kB):   512
Session Limit: 1024

APPLICATIONS

Customer Database
Scheduled by: Received Messages
Command Sequence:
Local CDB Return Data
>   Priority: 1
>   Routing Class: Standard
>   Transport Protocol: Generic
>   Message Size Calculation: Probability Distribution
>   Probability Distribution: 1024.0
>   Message Test Option: Set Message Text
>   Message Text: CDB Return Data
Received Messages:
>   CDB*

Inventory Database
Scheduled by: Received Messages
Command Sequence:
Local INV Return Data
>   Priority: 1
>   Routing Class: Standard
>   Transport Protocol: Generic
>   Message Size Calculation: Probability Distribution
>   Probability Distribution: 1024.0
>   Message Test Option: Set Message Text
>   Message Text: INV Return Data
Received Messages:
>   INV*

Order Processing
Scheduled by: Iteration
Arrival Times: Interarrival: EXP (5.0)
Command Sequence:
(T) CDB REQUEST FOR DATA
(T) INV REQUEST FOR DATA
CDB PROCESS DATA

Ship Order
Scheduled by: Iteration
Arrival Times: Interarrival: EXP (5.0)
Command Sequence:

(T) CDB REQUEST FOR DATA
(T) INV REQUEST FOR DATA
(T) CDB PROCESS DATA
(T) INV PROCESS DATA

Customer Inquiry
Scheduled by: Iteration
Arrival Times: Interarrival: EXP (5.0)
Command Sequence:
    (T) CDB REQUEST FOR DATA

Order Inquiry
Scheduled by: Iteration
Arrival Times: Interarrival: EXP (5.0)
Command Sequence:
    CDB REQUEST FOR DATA

Stock Status
Scheduled by: Iteration
Arrival Times: Interarrival: EXP (5.0)
Command Sequence:
    IVN REQUEST FOR DATA

COMMANDS

Transport Commands

CDB REQUEST FOR DATA
    Message: CDB REQUEST DATA
    Route: Random List
    To: Server 1

CDB PROCESS DATA
    Message: CDB PROCESS DATA
    Route: Random List
    To: Server 1

IVN REQUEST FOR DATA
    Message: IVN REQUEST DATA
    Route: Random List
    To: Server 2

INV PROCESS DATA
    Message: IVN PROCESS DATA
    Route: Random List
    To: Server 2

Answer Commands
CDB RETURN DATA

Receives messages:	CDB* (note the wildcard)
Answer messages:	CDB RETURN DATA

INV RETURN DATA

Receives messages:	INV* (note the wildcard)
Answer messages:	INV RETURN DATA

LINKS

CUSTOMER SERVICE LAN/DISTRIBUTION CENTER LAN
Type: CSMA/CD 802.3 Ethernet 10base5
Time to Fail: EXP (10.)
Time to Repair: EXP (1.0)

CUSTOMER SERVICE RING/ DISTRIBUTION CENTER RING
Type: Token Ring
          16 Mbps
Time to Failure EXP (10.)
Time to Repair EXP (1.0)

Router
Type: Cisco AGS+, V9.1(0.24)
Time to Failure: EXP (10.)
Time to Repair: EXP (1.0)

56 kbps line
Type: Point-to-Point 56 kbps
Time to Failure: EXP (5.0)
Time to Repair: EXP (2.0)

4.5 Data Compression Laboratory

by

Frances S. Grodzinsky and Ann Burroughs

Objective: This lab will familiarize you with the concept of data compression.

Brief Description: In Part I, using a Huffman coding tree, you will first write a program which simulates how a data compression program decodes a compressed input stream. In Part II, you will use the data compression utilities to evaluate data compression on different file types.

Audience: Computer science majors with networking and programming experience. Part II may be used alone for students with no programming experience.

Equipment: Access to compression utilities and language compilers.

Duration: Two weeks.

PROCEDURE

PART I: HUFFMAN CODING TREE

1. Consider the following probabilities:

Symbol	Probability
green	.31
blue	.26
red	.11
purple	.10
orange	.05
yellow	.08
brown	.09

a. Develop the Huffman coding tree for these symbols. Show the logic in a flowchart. Encode the message "purple blue red orange green yellow brown blue green green blue red green purple green red blue."

b. Using a Huffman compressed stream of 100 samples and the Hoffman coding you developed, what is the average number of bits per symbol? Using an arbitrary three-bit stream of 100 samples, what is the average number of bits per symbol? What is the theoretical percentage of compression? For your message, what percentage of compression did you achieve? How many bits would you need to send this message in a code where each symbol is represented by eight bits without compression?

c. Write a program which will decompress any bit string composed according this Huffman coding tree. Submit three test runs. Make sure that your program is well documented.[1]

d. With true data compression, you would have to unpack bytes to restore the message, because you would be sending bits to represent characters. How does this add to the complexity of the code? What issues would need to be addressed?

PART II: POPULAR FILE COMPRESSION UTILITIES[2]

Objective: This part of the lab will familiarize you with some common file compression utilities. These compression utilities can be used for backing up or coding files for transmission over a network. Also, you will learn how to connect to networked file services.

Procedure: You will compress three different types of files: word processing documents (.doc): graphic images (.gif), and DOS executables (.exe), using three popular compression utilities: PKZIP, the UNIX COMPRESS command, and a shareware compression utility from GNU software called GZip.[3] After recording the before and after sizes of these files, graph the average percentage of compression on each type of file for each compression utility.

You can download large files off the Internet and put them into a directory on the network.

How do I use PKZIP to compress a file?

To use PKZIP, you must know two things: the name of the file you want to compress, and where you want to put the compressed copy. Let's compress the files on the network to a directory on the hard drive on the computer you're using.

From within Windows, get to a command prompt (do not exit Windows, or you will be disconnected from the network). Create a directory named "backup" on the **C:** drive. Note the names of these files, as you will need to know them in order to run the compression program.

---

[1] For more advanced students: Write a program to receive an encoded message (a string of bits) and convert it to the original message. This means that you will have to construct the Huffman tree for this set of symbols. Your program will then use that information to decode the message.

[2] Thanks to Chris Beyer for developing and testing this part of the lab.

[3] Instructors may use any compression utility here.

To use PKZIP, simply type the following command at your prompt:

pkzip *destination_file file_to_ compress*

where destination_file is the name you want to give the resulting compressed file, and file_to_compress is the name of the file you want to compress (see Figure 1).

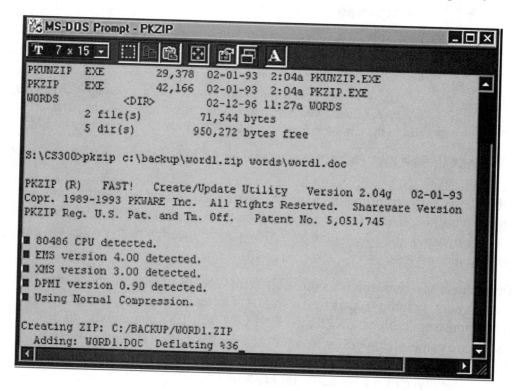

Figure 1

- Check the backup directory on the C: drive to determine the size of the compressed file, and the percentage of compression for each.

- Do this for each of the files in the three directories, computing the average percentage of compression for each type of file.

- Record these averages. You will later create a graph of the three different compression utilities and their compression rates on these same files.

How do I use UNIX compress and UNIX gzip to pack files?

To use either of these UNIX utilities, you must transfer these DOS files into your UNIX account. You may use DOS FTP to put these files into your account on a UNIX system.

NOTE: You can use the prompt and mput command in ftp to transfer more than one file at a time.

Once you have moved these files from DOS to UNIX, you may use the following commands to compress the files:

```
compress file_to_compress
```

When your prompt returns, UNIX is through compressing your file. If you check your directory listing, you will find that the original file word1.doc no longer exists and has been replaced by the compressed file (this file has a **.Z** extension tacked onto it). Whenever you see a file with a **.Z** extension, you know that it is a compressed file.

- Compress each of the files you transferred to your UNIX account; determine the size of the compressed file and the percentage of compression for each.

- Do this for each of the files and compute the average percentage of compression for each type of file.

- Record these averages. You will later create a graph of the three different compression utilities and their compression rates on these same files.

- Return the files to their original size by using the uncompress command.

  Type **uncompress** *compressed_filename* at your UNIX command prompt to make this happen.

  Once you have uncompressed the compressed files, you may use the following commands to GNU-Zip the files:

```
gzip file_to_compress
```

When your prompt returns, UNIX is through compressing your file.

- Use the GNU-Zip on each of the files you transferred to your UNIX account, determine the size of the compressed file and the percentage of compression for each.

- Do this for each of the files and compute the average percentage of compression for each type of file.

- After you have GNU-Zipped all the files from each directory, you may delete them from your account using the **rm** command.

  NOTE: To uncompress files that have been zipped with the GNU-Zip utility, use the command *gunzip compressed_file*.

FORMULATE RESULTS AND CONCLUSIONS

Now that you have all these numbers representing the compression ratios for different file types, create a chart[1] that graphically represents the differences among the utilities. Write your observations concerning the results. Discuss the differences not only in utilities but also in compressing the various file types.

---

[1] Students may use EXCEL or any spreadsheet for charts.

4.6 FTP 'Til You Drop

by

Frances S. Grodzinsky

Objective: To experience the differences in traffic on a closed LAN using FTP when the number of users is increased.

Brief Description: FTP (file transfer protocol) is the traditional UNIX method of transferring files, which has gained popularity as the de facto Internet standard for file transfer. File transfers are extended bursts of data, and this is a good process to use to analyze network traffic. Like most other network applications, the amount of processes demanding data affects the FTP rates. You can find general trends emerging that will tell you about networks, traffic flow and performance degradation.

Equipment: A closed LAN with its own server and a directory with files of varying sizes, including some big files! (Alternately, students may just FTP files of varying sizes from any site of their choosing.)

Audience: Data communications or networking students.

Duration: One week.

PROCEDURE:[1]

1. Log into your account, create a subdirectory and start a script file by typing

   ```
   script ftplab.scr
   ```

2. You will transfer six files of *varying sizes* from your server.[2] (Make sure that some are very large.) You may FTP from another site if it is more convenient.

   ```
   ftp servername (login as usual)
   ```

---

[1] Thanks to Darshan Toolsidass for revisions and for testing this lab.
[2] Instructors may want to create a directory on the server in order to choose the file sizes they want the students to use.

3. Change to the ftp directory **cd /ftplab**

   Turn off interactive mode **prompt**

   Get the unchanged executable **binary**

   Get all the files **mget ***

   End the session **bye**

   End the script **[Ctrl + D]**

4. Repeat the entire procedure with at least three other people doing this step simultaneously, or login on at least three other machines and FTP the files simultaneously using different subdirectories and script files (e.g., ftplab2.scr).

5. You should now have enough data to analyze network behavior. Print out the script files or view it using **more** to note down the necessary data.

Lab Report:

Using the following questions as a guide, analyze the data and draw your conclusions. Substantiate them *using graphs, tables or figures*.

- Generally speaking, what will maximize throughput?

- Generally speaking, what will slow it down the most?

- How many people do you see logged in?

- Are there any invisible users? Get onto sunflower and type **who.**

- What is the theoretical transfer rate over Ethernet?

- Which files came in quickest? Why? How does this compare to the theoretical transfer rate?

- Did any other factors affect the network traffic on this LAN when you were running your tests?

- What kind of relationship does the number of connections have to network traffic flow? Why?

- What would you suggest to the authors of a new, improved FTP program?

4.7 Using Ping to Measure Response Time

by

*Frances S. Grodzinsky
and Ann Burroughs*

Objective: This lab will familiarize you with the network utility ***ping***. Ping is used for network testing, measurement, and management. The *ping* program uses ICMP (Internet Control Message Protocol) to send an ECHO_REQUEST to elicit an ICMP ECHO_RESPONSE from the specified host.

Brief Description: You will use ping to test some sites on the Internet, then record the average response time for each site. Determine the approximate physical distance in miles between your university and each site. You will probably need an atlas, unless you can find appropriate maps on the Web. Ping five sites from the United States, five from Europe, five from developing countries (make sure your sites are in the country and not created in the U.S. or elsewhere) and one from on campus. The usual use for *ping* is to determine if a particular host or Internet gateway is alive. But *ping* has many useful features, including the ability to report the route the ECHO_REQUEST took on its journey across the network, and the ability to report the round-trip elapsed time for the two datagrams (ECHO_REQUEST and ECHO_RESPONSE). In a nutshell, ping sends a message to a networked computer and requests a response. It waits for the response and displays the amount of time the response took.

Audience: Computer and information science majors.

Equipment: A network with access to Netscape, Internet Explorer and the WWW, and a spreadsheet program.

Duration: One week.

PROCEDURE:

1. You will use ping to test some sites on the Internet, then record the average response time for each site.

2. Determine the approximate physical distance in miles between your university and each site. You will probably need an atlas, unless you can find appropriate maps on the Web. Ping five sites from the United States, five from Europe, five from developing countries (make sure your sites are in the country and not created in the U.S. or elsewhere) and one from on campus. The

usual use for *ping* is to determine if a particular host or Internet gateway is alive. But *ping* has many useful features, including the ability to report the route the ECHO_REQUEST took on its journey across the network, and the ability to report the round-trip elapsed time for the two datagrams (ECHO_REQUEST and ECHO_RESPONSE). In a nutshell, ping sends a message to a networked computer and requests a response. It waits for the response and displays the amount of time the response took.

3. Use an XY graph to display the relationship between response time and physical distance at one time of day.

4. Use another XY graph to display the relationship (if any) between distance and packet loss.

5. Now ping these same sites at another time of day. Make sure the times are quite far apart (e.g., 9 am and 5 pm). You may even try the same time on a weekday and a weekend day. Generate a graph for each time of day showing the minimum, maximum, and average response times for every site. Then generate a comparative graph of the average response times for every site for both times of day. Make sure to identify the sites on the graph (e.g., provide a key).

6. Write a paragraph recording your observations about locations, times of day, and time zones. Was it difficult to find host sites in developing countries? What conclusions can you draw from your observations?

7. Hand in your observations, graphs and a spreadsheet along with the raw data. Did the numbers come out the way you thought they would? *Remember* the response time is not so much a function of machine speed as it is a function of the number of connections between your computer and the machine you are testing.

HELPFUL INFORMATION:

HOW DO I IDENTIFY LOCATIONS?

One way to identify these locations is to use an Internet search, which will return URLs for which you can interpret the host's location (for instance mit is Massachusetts Institute of Technology, or wustl is Washington University at St. Louis; fr means France; au means Australia; kr means Korea, etc.). If you are looking for hosts in Europe, you could use search keywords which would be likely to give you European hosts (for instance, *chateau* or *Thames*).

Finally, you can find host addresses in many Internet directories, such as the *Internet Yellow Pages*.

All World Wide Web sites that you can access with Netscape are hosted on computers that will respond to ping. You can get the hostname of these WWW computers by looking at the Location: box at the top of the Netscape screen.

How do I use ping to get the average response time for a site?

To use ping, simply type the following command at your UNIX prompt: ping *hostname* where hostname is the name of the computer on the Internet you want to test.

If the computer does not exist, ping will display an error message saying the hostname you specified cannot be found.

If ping finds the hostname you have specified, it will let you know that it is alive.

```
━                    [Inactive FTP PING Utility]                    ▼ ▲
Usage: ping [-t] [-a] [-n count] [-l size] [-f] [-i TTL] [-v TOS]
            [-r count] [-s count] [[-j host-list] ¦ [-k host-list]]
            [-w timeout] destination-list

Options:
    -t                  Ping the specifed host until interrupted.
    -a                  Resolve addresses to hostnames.
    -n count            Number of echo requests to send.
    -l size             Send buffer size.
    -f                  Set Don't Fragment flag in packet.
    -i TTL              Time To Live.
    -v TOS              Type Of Service.
    -r count            Record route for count hops.
    -s count            Timestamp for count hops.
    -j host-list        Loose source route along host-list.
    -k host-list        Strict source route along host-list.
    -w timeout          Timeout in milliseconds to wait for each reply.
```

A sample *ping* command would be:

```
ping -s www.humboldt.edu -l 64 -n 10
```

This command asks to ping the host www.humboldt.edu with packets 64 bytes long and to repeat the process 10 times. The -s flag is necessary for gathering the timing statistics we want. If you do not want to use the -n switch, you can terminate the test with CTRL C.

For example, after ping has run through 10 trials, terminate the test by holding down the **CTRL** key and tapping the letter **C**. Ping should print out the average response time on its last line of output (see next page).

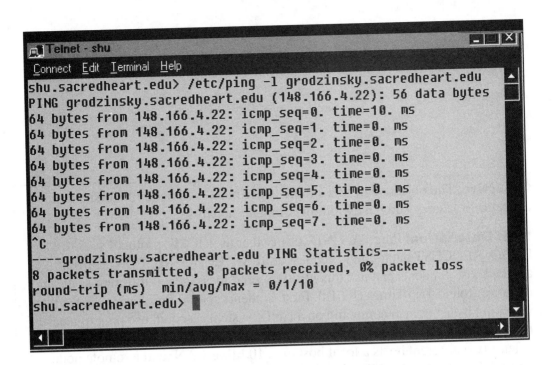

```
Telnet - shu
Connect  Edit  Terminal  Help
shu.sacredheart.edu> /etc/ping -l grodzinsky.sacredheart.edu
PING grodzinsky.sacredheart.edu (148.166.4.22): 56 data bytes
64 bytes from 148.166.4.22: icmp_seq=0. time=10. ms
64 bytes from 148.166.4.22: icmp_seq=1. time=0. ms
64 bytes from 148.166.4.22: icmp_seq=2. time=0. ms
64 bytes from 148.166.4.22: icmp_seq=3. time=0. ms
64 bytes from 148.166.4.22: icmp_seq=4. time=0. ms
64 bytes from 148.166.4.22: icmp_seq=5. time=0. ms
64 bytes from 148.166.4.22: icmp_seq=6. time=0. ms
64 bytes from 148.166.4.22: icmp_seq=7. time=0. ms
^C
----grodzinsky.sacredheart.edu PING Statistics----
8 packets transmitted, 8 packets received, 0% packet loss
round-trip (ms)  min/avg/max = 0/1/10
shu.sacredheart.edu>
```

4.8 Pinging to Understand Latency

by

Kamyar Dezhgosha

Objective: The objective of this simple experiment is to better understand the concepts of latency and bandwidth in computer networks.

Brief Description: Ping is a UNIX utility that uses ICMP protocol's ECHO_REQUEST datagram to request an ICMP ECHO_RESPONSE from another host. Students can use this utility to send messages of different sizes and measure Round Trip Times (RTTs). First, students should familiarize themselves with ping by using man command on a UNIX system. Second, use ping to measure RTT for messages of 8, 16, 32, 64, 256, and 512 bytes. They should try pinging to at least two different hosts a local host on a 10 Mbps LAN, and a remote node through Internet and 1.5 Mbps links. They should observe a measurable increase in RTT for remote Internet hosts as one increases message size. Students may break down the RTT into its components (Propagation + Transmit + Queue) to discuss the effect of distance and message size and their relation to latency and bandwidth.

Audience: Students in computer networking and data communication who are familiar with UNIX and have a basic knowledge of Round Trip Time in computer networks.

Equipment: UNIX and Internet access.

Duration: Either as a two-hour in-lab work or one week out-of-lab.

PROCEDURE:

1. Use "man" command to familiarize yourself with "ping."

2. Use "ping" to measure Round Trip Time (RTT) for messages of 8, 16, 32, 64, 256, … bytes. It is better to measure between five to 30 times for each message size, depending on the situation and availability of time, and use the average.

3. Graph message size versus RTT for two hosts on a LAN and two nodes on a WAN.

Lab Report:

Write a report that discusses RTT in terms of its components (Startup Overhead + Propagation + Transmit + Queue). Also, discuss the effects of distance, message size, and their relationship with bandwidth and latency.

4.9 Traceroute

by

Ann Burroughs

Objective: Students will gain a better understanding of the organization of the Internet within the U.S. They will also experimentally attempt to derive a relationship between packet transit times and number of hops, as well as between packet transit times and number of backbones involved in the route. They will analyze raw data and present results.

Brief Description: Using traceroute, students examine the path an ICMP message takes from source to destination. They then hypothesize about the relationship between transit times, number of hops, distances and backbone transfers. This can be done by two-student teams.

Audience: Students with Internet experience, an introduction to Internet architecture, including routing and backbones, and a knowledge of spreadsheets sufficient to enter raw data and manipulate it for correlation analysis.

Equipment: Access to traceroute (Telnet is fine).

Duration: Two hours for the experiment; one week for the write-up.

PROCEDURE:

While it might be useful to think about an Internet "backbone," there is really no single entity which has such a function. In the late 1980s the National Science Foundation, which had been sponsoring what we can think of as a backbone network across the country, began to transition that service to private entities such as ANS, MCI, Sprint, BBN, PSI, etc. These commercial entities each maintain very high speed, large-bandwidth interstate networks at least partially for Internet purposes. These companies are Internet Service Providers to smaller ISPs who pay to access these data routes, as well as to corporate customers wanting Internet access in the geographical locations directly served by the large company. Of course, the smaller ISPs in turn provide access to customers, including other ISPs, in locations distributed around a smaller geographical area.

There are a number of big players in this nationwide backbone market. The specific topologies of their networks differ—some concentrate on the east coast, some in middle America, some on the west—but they typically span the country.

Obviously, in order for a user attached to one of them to communicate with a user attached to another, the backbones need to be interconnected. This occurs in several locations throughout the U.S. at so-called MAEs (Metropolitan Area Ethernets), NAPs (Network Access Points) or IEPs (Internet Exchange Points). The important ones are MAE-WEST (San Jose), MAE-EAST (Washington, D.C.), Chicago, and New York. At such locations, the big players interconnect.

For an excellent presentation of the backbones of the Internet, see www.boardwatch.com/ISP/backbone.html. In addition to a map, you can find details about each of the national-level providers of Internet service.

On your UNIX system, there is a program called *traceroute*. If you read the main pages for *traceroute*, you can learn the details of how it teases from the *tcp/ip* routers along a path between two Internet hosts the details of that path. You can also read the warning that "This program is intended for use in network testing, measurement and management. It should be used primarily for manual fault isolation. Because of the load it could impose on the network, you should not use traceroute during normal operations or from automated scripts."

Here's a sample:

```
axe> traceroute www.mit.edu
traceroute to ANXIETY-CLOSET.MIT.EDU (18.181.0.21), 30 hops
max, 40 byte packets
 1  hsu32768.humboldt.edu (137.150.128.1)2ms 2ms 2ms
 2  137.145.173.100 (137.145.173.100)20ms 23ms 26ms
 3  SWRL-ATM-GW.CSU.NET (204.102.243.111)32ms 43ms 51ms
 4  bordercore1-hssi1-0.Bloomington.mci.net(166.48.173.253)
    51ms 41ms 43ms
 5  * bordercore2-loopback.Atlanta.mci.ne(166.48.48.1)140ms
    79ms
 6  core2-hssi-2.Boston.mci.net (204.70.1.101)116ms 148ms
    155ms
 7  core2-hssi-2.Boston.mci.net (204.70.1.101)139ms 137ms
    142ms
 8  borderx2-fddi-1.Boston.mci.net (204.70.179.68)143ms
    142ms 138 ms
 9  nearnet.Boston.mci.net(204.70.179.122)373ms 120ms 355ms
10  ihtfp.mit.edu (192.233.33.3) 136ms 134ms 129ms
11  W20-RTR-FDDI.MIT.EDU(18.168.0.8)124ms 171ms 126ms
12  ANXIETY-CLOSET.MIT.EDU (18.181.0.21)120ms 134ms
120ms
```

You can see that the route between *axe* and *anxiety-closet* at MIT in Boston is 12 hops long. The first four hops are relatively local, as are the final three. You can also see that there are five hops along the MCI backbone. Evidently, this route did not require multiple backbones, since we do not see evidence of PSInet or Sprintlink or ANS in the *traceroute* results.

Here's another example, this time to the University of Texas at Austin:

```
axe> traceroute www.uta.edu
traceroute to cwis.uta.edu (129.107.56.17),30 hops max,
```

```
40 byte packets
 1 hsu32768.humboldt.edu (137.150.128.1) 2ms 3ms 2ms
 2 137.145.173.100 (137.145.173.100) 18ms 16ms 17ms
 3 SWRL-ATM-GW.CSU.NET (204.102.243.111)31ms 30ms 29ms
 4 bordercore1-hssi1-0.Bloomington.mci.net(166.48.173.253)
   42ms 36ms 34ms
 5 somerouter.sprintlink.net (206.157.77.42)127ms 215ms
   338ms
 6 somerouter.sprintlink.net (206.157.77.42)295ms 324ms
   329ms
 7 sl-fw-6-H2/0-T3.sprintlink.net(144.228.10.29)61ms 66ms
   73ms
 8 sl-fw-15-F0/0.sprintlink.net (144.228.30.15)72ms 73ms
   67ms
 9 sl-uoftx-1-H0/0-T3.sprintlink.net (144.228.135.34)69ms
   94ms 89ms
10 ut5-h2-0.the.net (129.117.16.241)101ms 83ms 78ms
11 utd6-h1-0.the.net (129.117.24.18)117ms 101ms 103ms
12 uta1-s1.the.net (129.117.20.98)129ms 123ms 166ms
13 nbdavb93.uta.edu (129.107.1.251)142ms 145ms 104ms
14 129.107.252.250 (129.107.252.250)94ms 110ms 113ms
15 cwis.uta.edu (129.107.56.17)200ms 155ms 108ms
```

This time you can observe the transition between MCINet and SprintLinkNet backbones. You can also see how many hops were required at the far end after the last SprintLinkNet hop as the route went through more local routers (looks like a Texas Higher Education network of some sort, doesn't it?).

1. For this experiment, use a sample size of at least 50 (150 would be ideal). Try to spread your sample geographically around the entire lower 48 states, making sure you cover all areas. How you determine which Internet sites to use is your decision. Using a search for a geographically specific topic will usually yield several useful sites.

2. For each of your sites, *ping* the site 10 times and record the average. Then **immediately** run *traceroute* to the site, and record or capture the results. Don't do all the *pings* first and then all the *traceroutes*, because we want the *ping* and the *traceroute* to the same site to be done before any routing tables might reasonably change (although, of course, we can't guarantee that they won't).

    Now, analyze your results. What is the correlation between average *ping* time and hop count? Between distance and hop count? Between average *ping* time and Internet Service Provider transitions?

3. In order to report your results, you'll need to do correlation analyses. The easiest way to do this is to use the PEARSON function in Excel, which should

give you a coefficient of correlation between -1 and 1. Here's the interpretation of a positive result (negative correlation has a similar scale):

near 0   no correlation

.40–.59   weak correlation

.60–.79   moderate correlation

.80–.89   strong correlation

.90–1   very strong correlation

Report your results on a spreadsheet. Use the format below for your raw data so that the entire class results can be combined easily. Show all three correlation coefficients. Graph all three relationships using an XY scatter graph. Write a report in which you describe your experiment and present your results. Make sure that, as part of your report, there is a listing of your raw results. Also include a map of the lower 48 states with your 25 sites clearly marked. As part of the package which you turn in, include a disk with the spreadsheet containing your data.

A	B	C	D	E	F	G	H	I	J	K
1	Your name(s) here									
2										
3	Site name	Site IP address	Site city	Site state		Distance in miles	Distance in kilometers	Average ping time	Number of hops	Number of ISP transitions
4										
5	Start entering data	in this row								
6										

4.10 Sniffer Lab (Capture the Packet)

by

Bruce Elenbogen

Objective: This lab is intended to show students real traffic.

Brief Description: Students will see various types of packets and get a sense of the size of a packet and the frequency at which they are sent. This lab will show the utilization of the network and give students a sense of the internal packets used by the network to keep itself running. Unfortunately, this type of knowledge can be misused, so a discussion of sniffer misuse is essential.

Audience: Knowledge of FTP and HDLC makes the lab more meaningful, but students do no need any special knowledge.

Equipment: Networked PC lab, Internet access, LAN Windows Sniffer; if the LAN is connected to various types of networks, so much the better.

Duration: One week.

PROCEDURE:

INSTRUCTIONS FOR USE OF SNIFFER.

1. Boot PC and escape to DOS.

2. CD LW

3. LANW

   a. There are three basic modes we will use for LAN windows:

      r—real time

      t— statistics

      e—examine

   b. Begin in real-time mode. Answer the following questions:

      1. Identify four different types of packets

         1 Length (bits) Type Sent from Sent to

         2 Length (bits) Type Sent from Sent to

3 Length (bits) Type Sent from Sent to

4 Length (bits) Type Sent from Sent to

2. By examining the packets, name four different types of machines/networks on the network (e.g., Sun):

1.   2.

3.   4.

c. Examine packets

Hit e to examine packets. You can then choose a packet to look at in detail by using the arrow keys (page up/page down) and hitting return.

1. Examine an IP (Internet) packet. Write down the contents below.

2. Examine an 802.2 (Novell) packet. Write down the contents below.

d. Hit t to see statistics.

1. What is the average number of packets on the network (estimate)?

2. What is the bandwidth of network?

3. What is the average size of packets on the network (estimate)?

4. What is the background line utilization (estimate)?

e. Experiment: Have the instructor or another student FTP a file.

1. Examine the packets (they are indicated by FTP). Display one below.

2. What is the traffic increase caused by the FTP?

3. What is the line utilization during the FTP?

f. What other experiments can you suggest for the sniffer?

4.11 Ethernet vs. Token Bus

by

Bruce Elenbogen

Objective: This lab is intended to instruct students about what affects performance of a network. A secondary goal is the comparison of a token bus versus Ethernet as congestion increases.

Brief Description: You are the network manager of the Xerax company. The company wants to put in a little network to connect the offices of the executives of the company, namely: President, Vice-president, Secretary, Treasurer, and, of course, the Network Manager. Each person currently has a machine on his/her desk, and you will be purchasing a server which will be connected to each computer. You have a choice to make on the type of the network (Ethernet or token bus), and you can use Comnet to simulate both types and make an informed choice.

Audience: Students with a knowledge of token and CSMA/CD protocols.

Equipment: Comnet[1] software.

Duration: Two weeks.

[1] Comnet is a product of CACI, La Jolla, CA.

PROCEDURE:

PHYSICAL CONSTRAINTS:

Regardless of your choice of network, each machine will talk only to the server. The server will then answer the querying machine. To simulate this, create one traffic icon which goes from one computer to the server, and one icon going from the server to the computer. Put a line from the first icon to the second, and any message from the computer to the server will trigger a return message from the server back to the computer.

TRAFFIC TO THE SERVER:

The traffic to the server will be a uniform distribution from one to 1000 bytes long.

The interarrival time for the clients will be a uniform distribution from one to 1000 seconds.

TRAFFIC FROM THE SERVER:

The traffic from the server will be a uniform distribution, from 1 to 2 k. Make this traffic triggered from traffic to the server from the same computer.

LINK—ETHERNET

Use the default values of the CSMA/CD. Set the frame Min to 64 and the frame Max to 512 bytes. There is only one QPriority, and that is 1. Set the frame error to 0.05 (that is very high but makes for more fun).

LINK—TOKENBUS

Choose Token. Set the slot size to 10 ms and the time to change slots to 1 ms. Set the frame Min to 64 and the frame Max to 1500 bytes. There is only one QPriority, and that is 1. Set the frame error to 0.05.

COMPUTERS

Each computer has a buffer of 1024 and a buffer cutoff of 1000. The time for each action of the computer (right-hand column) is 10 ms.

THE SERVER

The Server has a buffer of 2000 bytes and a cutoff of 1000 bytes. The delay for each operation of the server is only one ms.

ROUTING

Choose Min penalty, with ACK packet of three bytes, ReXmit of 500 and Rtng update of 5000.

TRANSFER RATE

(On the link) Experiment with link speeds of 1 kbps.

Lab Report:

Print of a copy of your network, all applicable plots and a one-page analysis of your networks, including your conclusions on what to set up. You may take into account any data you feel will be relevant. To make a copy of the screen, choose the P icon on the upper right-hand corner of any of the Comnet programs (comnetin, comnet-an, or complot). This will cause a printable file to be created (the default name is print1.ps). Now type lpr -Psparc <your ps file name>, and a hard copy will appear from the laser printer.

Run a 30-minute simulation using Comnet as opposed to comnetan, since the simulation will then run much faster.

BONUS QUESTIONS

Assume growth.

—At what growth will your answer to the above change?
(Simulate growth by decreasing the link speed)

Assume more distribution of programs..

—At what traffic level will the answer to the above change?
(Simulate more distribution (less traffic) by increasing the link speed.)

STEP-BY-STEP CREATION OF THE SIMULATION FOR VERSIONS < 3.0

First you need to run comnetin.

1. Create the server.

   a. Choose a node icon (rectangular symbol).

      1. Under EDIT, pull down detail and fill in the details of the server.

2. Create one client.

   a. Choose a node icon (rectangular symbol).

      1. Under EDIT, pull down detail and fill in the details of one of the clients.

3. Create the link.

   a. Choose the link icon (hexagon).

      1. Under EDIT, pull down detail and fill in the details of link.

4. Connect the server and client to the link.

   a. Choose the line.

      1. Draw a line from the client to the link and from the server to the link.

5. Make four more clients.

   a. Select the client.

      1. Under EDIT choose clone and duplicate the link.

6. Create traffic

   a. Select the traffic icon, which is message passing (diamond).

      1. Under EDIT, choose detail to make the traffic to the server.

   b. Select the line.

      1. Draw a line from the client to the traffic icon and from the traffic icon to the server.

   c. Select the traffic icon.

      1. Clone the icon four more times.

      2. Use a line to make traffic from each client to the server.

   d. Select the traffic icon.

      1. Make it the triggered traffic from the server back to the client.

    2. Clone it four times.

    3. Connect each of the these five icons from the server to the clients.

7.   Set the run time.

    a. Under Run

      1. Set run time for five minutes, 10 seconds (to start).

      2. Set plot time from 10 seconds to 310 seconds.

      3. Be sure to check plot.

8.   Under EDIT, choose verify.

    If it verifies, save it. (The names will be converted to all capitals, regardless of what you type.)

9.   Run comnetan <your file name>.

10.   Run complot < your filename>.

    If your plot looks reasonable, change the run time to 30 minutes and use Comnet instead of comnetan.

4.12 Performance Measurement in Sockets Communication

by

Kamyar Dezhgosha

Objective: The objective of this programming assignment is to go one step beyond using sockets for communication between machines, and to learn about performance metrics such as latency and throughput in computer networks.

Brief Description: Sockets are interprocess communication mechanisms that allow processes to communicate with each other, even if they are on different machines. Students will use Internet Sockets to send different-sized messages between two UNIX machines and measure latency and throughput. First, students should familiarize themselves with Internet Sockets and client/server programming [1–2]. Second, write programs using sockets to send a one-byte message from a machine to another machine, and have the other machine return the message. This process is repeated in a loop 1000 times, and the average round-trip time (latency) for a one-byte message is calculated. Third, students increase the message size to 1kB, 2kB, 4kB, 8kB, and 16kB. They measure the round-trip times for each case, and determine the effective throughput for each message size. Finally, plotting throughput vs. message size will give them an insight into the relationship between latency, bandwidth, and application requirements (message size).

Audience: Students in computer networks class who are familiar with UNIX and C programming, and optionally UNIX Sockets.

Equipment: UNIX network (LAN).

Duration: It may be assigned as a two- to three-week project or lab assignment with the first half of the assignment (round-trip time for one-byte message) due in the middle of the period (in seven to ten days).

PROCEDURE:

1. Use references such as [1–2] to familiarize yourself with Sockets.

2. Write client/server programs using Sockets to send a one-byte message from one machine to another, and have the other machine return the message.

3. Repeat the above process in a loop 1000 times, and calculate the average round-trip time (latency) for a one-byte message.

125

4. Increase the message size in the above program to 1kB, 2kB, 4kB, 8kB, and 16kB. Discuss any problems encountered in this process, and measure the round-trip times for each case. Determine the effective throughput for each message size.

5. Plot throughput vs. message size, and discuss the results.

REFERENCES:

1. Glass, G. (1993), *Unix for Programmers and Users*, Prentice Hall, Englewood Cliffs, NJ.

2. Commer, D. E., and Stevens, D. L. (1994), *Internetworking with TCP/IP*, Volume III, Prentice Hall, Upper Saddle River, NJ.

4.13 Impact of Traffic Patterns in Communication Networks: M/M/1, M/D/1, D/D/1

by

J.C. Olabe and M.A. Olabe

Objective: This laboratory is designed to illustrate the impact of traffic patterns in overall network performance. A sequence of simulations is designed to help the student: 1) identify the differences between average and instantaneous network performance; 2) evaluate the effects of the packet interarrival distribution; and 3) evaluate the effects of the packet size distribution

Brief Description: This project studies the instantaneous time average packet-delay and buffer occupancy of a two-node, single-link network under three traffic distributions. The traffic distributions are selected to create queuing processes for which analytical solutions exist. These processes correspond to the M/M/1, M/D/1, and D/D/1 queuing systems, and their analytical solutions will be used to validate the results obtained during simulation. A total of 27 simulations (nine per network) are implemented. The three networks are simulated under a similar set of traffic intensities (10% to 90%, in increments of 10%.) For each simulation, the instantaneous packet delay, buffer occupancy, as well as average link utilization, average delay, and average buffer occupancy are recorded. The recorded average results are plotted along with their analytical counterparts, and conclusions are drawn about the effect of changing the packet size distribution (M/M/1 vs. M/D/1), and of changing the packet interarrival distribution (M/D/1 vs. D/D/1). The simulation results are also used to draw conclusions about the analytical averages and the simulation instantaneous results.

Audience: Electrical engineering, telecommunications, and networking students at the junior or senior level, with a good background in probability and statistics, queuing theory, and the use of simulation in network analysis and performance evaluation.

Equipment: MathCAD is used to plot analytical expected values as well as instantaneous simulation range values. COMNET III is used to model and simulate three simple two-node networks.

Duration: Two laboratory sessions: 1) modeling and simulation of 27 simple networks (three traffic patterns with nine traffic intensities each); and 2) analysis of simulation average results and comparison with analytical solutions, and evaluation of simulation instantaneous value ranges. Finally, one to two hours will be dedicated to documenting the project in a written report.

PROCEDURE:

1. **Network modeling:** This experiment requires the creation of 27 COMNET III files to describe a simple network operating under three different traffic distributions (M/M/1, M/D/1, and D/D/1) and nine different traffic intensities (10% to 90%, in increments of 10%). The topology and operation of all files is similar and includes two processing nodes (source and destination) and one point-to-point link. The processing nodes will be defined with ideal characteristics (default values). The link will also be defined by its default value. Its transmission rate will be set to 1 Mbps. This capacity, along with a packet size of 1kb, creates the service rate m = 1000 pck/sec.

2. **Traffic modeling:** A single message source icon connected to source node is used to define the traffic of each network. The message size is set to 125 bytes (1kb) with deterministic distribution (M/D/1 and D/D/1) or with exponential distribution (M/M/1). The packet interarrival distribution and time are used to define the type of traffic, as well as the traffic intensity (100 packets per second is equivalent to 10% traffic intensity, 200 pck/sec is 20%, etc.).

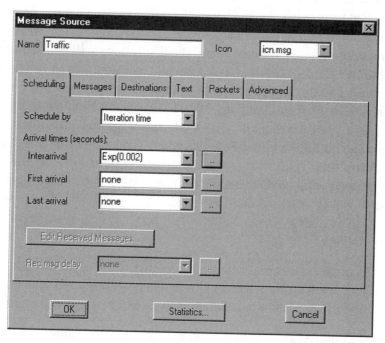

Figure 1 Defining Traffic Characteristics

3. **Report definition and data collection:** Before executing each simulation, the relevant report and plots need to be activated. These include the Packet delay statistics, Packets in transit statistics, and average link utilization. In addition, the instantaneous packets in transit and instantaneous packet delay plots and statistics need to be activated.

4. **Simulation:** Since these networks reach their steady-state operation rapidly, the simulation process is both simple and fast. Different networks could be run for different lengths, since they work at different traffic intensity points.

A good rule of thumb is to allow a substantial number of packets (5000–10000) to be simulated.

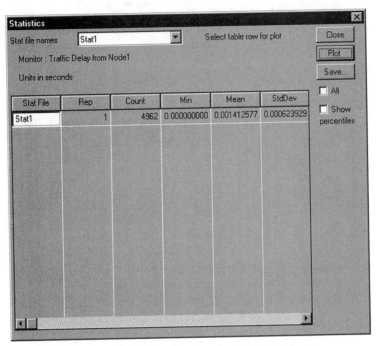

Figure 2 Collected Data for 4962 Packets

1. **Analytical solution vs. simulation results:** A MathCAD file containing the three analytical equations for packet delay {E(T)} and buffer occupancy {E(n)} for M/M/1, M/D/1, and D/D/1} queues is created. This file will be used as a reference to validate the 27 sets of values obtained during simulation.

2. **Evaluation of instantaneous value ranges:** The analytical models offer an estimate of the expected averages of delay and buffer occupancy. COMNET III, in addition to its own simulated averages, offers an instantaneous record of delay and buffer occupancy. These instantaneous plots will be used to critically evaluate the meaning of average values, and the risk to ignore the minimum-maximum ranges associated with these averages.

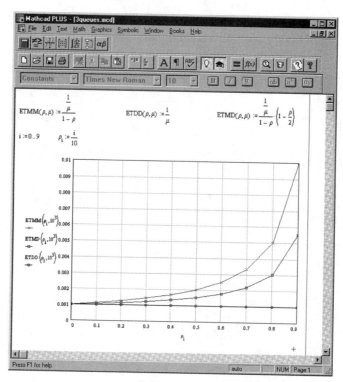

Figure 3 Analytical Packet Delay Models

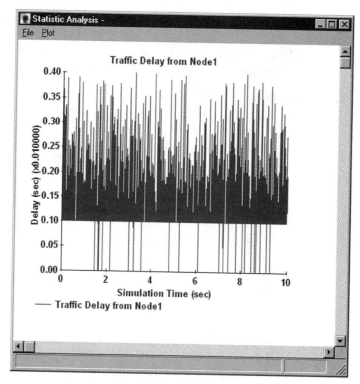

Figure 4 Instantaneous Packet Delay

3. **Conclusions and documentation:** The written report will describe: 1) the common characteristics of the COMMET III files created; 2) the traffic parameters used to model the three different queuing models and the nine different traffic intensities; 3) the analytical equations used to evaluate the accuracy of simulation delay and buffer occupancy data; 4) a critical evaluation of the 27 report files obtained from simulation; 5) a critical evaluation of the effects of interarrival and packet size distributions; and 6) a critical evaluation of the differences between the analytical average values and the range of instantaneous values obtained during simulation.

To be included with the written report:

A. Summary of data used in 27 *.c3 data files

B. Printout of 27 report files containing:

Simulation length

Packet delay statistics

Packets in transit statistics

Average link utilization

C. Real-time plots of instantaneous buffer occupancy (27 plots)

D. Real-time plots of instantaneous packet delay (27 plots)

E. MathCAD plots of analytical models for packet delay $\{E(T)\}$ and buffer occupancy $\{E(n)\}$ for M/M/1, M/D/1, and D/D/1 queues

F. MathCAD plots of recorded simulation data for instantaneous $E(T)$, instantaneous $E(n)$, and average, minimum, and maximum values for $E(T)$ and $E(n)$

4.14 Modeling, Parametrization, and Validation of Real Network Traffic

by

J.C. Olabe and M.A. Olabe

Objective: This laboratory helps the student: 1) understand the need to collect traffic data from a communications network in order to model it using probabilistic methods; 2) evaluate the adverse consequences of using inappropriate traffic models in simulation studies; and 3) experience the process of traffic modeling and validation in a case-study exercise.

Brief Description: The students are provided with several files containing records of actual network traffic.[1] This laboratory is divided into three well-defined sections: 1) traffic modeling (given the general shape of the histogram obtained from the traffic data, one or more function candidates are selected from a set of well-known probability density functions used in traffic modeling); 2) traffic parametrization (using numerical methods, sets of parameters are obtained to minimize the error between the real traffic data and the candidate distribution functions); and 3) model validation (the degree of similarity between the real traffic and the probabilistic model is formally evaluated using statistical methods such as the chi-square method).

Audience: Electrical engineering, telecommunications, and networking students at the junior or senior level, with a good background in probability and statistics, queuing theory, and the use of simulation in network analysis and performance evaluation.

Equipment: MathCAD is used throughout this project to graphically display traffic characteristics, automatically determine the optimum parameters for the probabilistic models, and implement the chi-square method of statistical validation.

Duration: Two laboratory sessions: 1) graphical representation of traffic characteristics using histograms and selection of candidate probabilistic models; and 2) automatic parametrization of selected models and formal validation of candidate models for selected levels of confidence. Finally, one to two hours will be dedicated to document the project in a written report.

---

[1] These files may be obtained via e-mail from jolabe@cbu.edu or from the prenhall.com Web site.

PROCEDURE:

1. **Input traffic data and analysis files:** To implement this experiment, the students are provided with a group of MathCAD files to be used in the processes of traffic modeling, parametrization, and statistical validation. These files will be modified throughout the experiments to incorporate new probabilistic models, including exponential, gamma, normal, log-normal, Weibull, beta, Person V, and Person VI distributions. In addition, the students are provided with three files containing records of three traffic signals. These traffic files are the object of modeling and validation of this experiment. Figure 1 shows the time evolution of one of the traffic signals.

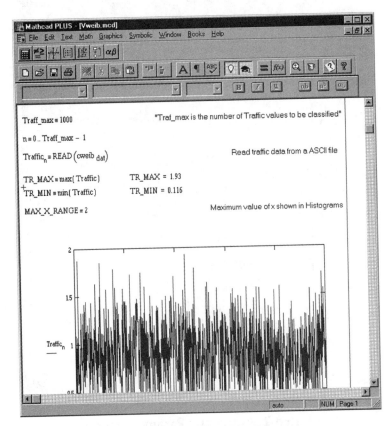

Figure 1 Time Evolution of Traffic Intensity

2. **Traffic modeling and reference model set:** The procedure used in the probabilistic modeling of traffic is the graphic representation of its histogram and the identification of a probability distribution that will provide a similar histogram. For this purpose, the students are required to incorporate in the MathCAD files provided the pdf (probability density function) of a set of distributions widely used in traffic modeling tasks, including exponential, gamma, normal, log-normal, Weibull, beta, Person V, and Person VI distributions.

3. **Automatic parametrization using numerical methods:** For each problem signal, a histogram is first obtained. Based on the general shape of the histogram, a group of candidate distributions can be selected. For example, if the

traffic histogram has a skewed bell shape, the Weibull, log-normal, and gamma distributions are candidate model distributions. After this selection has been made, the students determine the optimum parameters of the candidate distributions. This process is implemented by first calculating the mean and variance of the traffic signal and then solving a system of equations particular to each distribution. MathCAD allows the students to use numerical methods for the resolution of such systems. Figure 2 shows an example of the numerical resolution of one such system and the graphic representation of the traffic histogram and the calculated model.

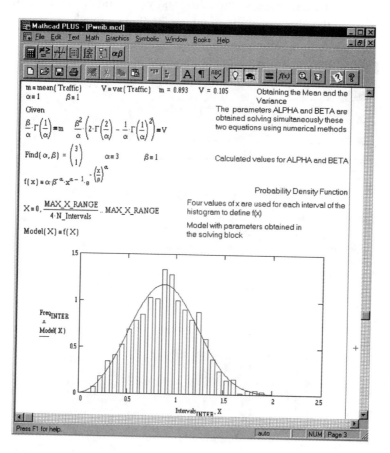

Figure 2 Automatic Parametrization

4. **Visual evaluation of candidate models:** The process of model validation starts with the creation of a histogram of the candidate model. This histogram is calculated integrating the pdf within the same intervals used in the original traffic model. Figure 3 shows the creation of one such histogram and the graphic comparison of both data and model histograms. If these histograms differ enough to be evident to the untrained eye, the model is rejected. Otherwise, a formal statistical validation is performed.

5. **Implementation of statistical validation—the chi-square method:** The final process of traffic modeling is the statistical validation of the model. This process measures the difference between the histogram obtained from the traffic data and the probabilistic model, and compares their difference with

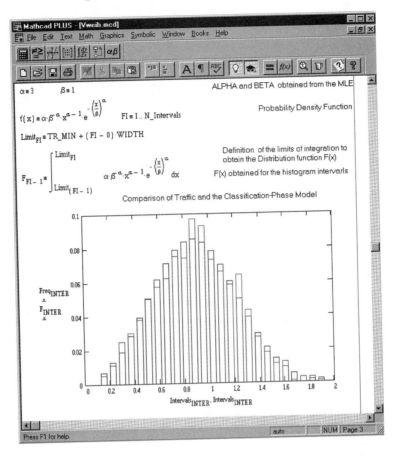

Figure 3 Visual Inspection of Candidate Models

that of two equal stochastic processes. If the difference is greater than that expected, the model is rejected, otherwise, the model is adopted. Several statistical procedures have been devised for this purpose. One that is widely established is the chi-square method. A MathCAD file is used to perform this method. Figure 4 shows an example of the chi-square method applied to two histograms, traffic and model, with 24 degrees of freedom (25 histogram bars) and a 95% level of confidence.

6. **Replication of the analysis for traffic data sets B and C:** The procedure is repeated for the other two sets of traffic data.

7. **Conclusions and documentation:** The written report will describe: 1) the MathCAD files used and created to model, obtain parameters, and validate traffic data; 2) the main types of probabilistic models, based on the shape of the histogram; 3) relevant steps in determining the candidate distributions using the histogram of the data; 4) methods used to determine the best parameters of the probabilistic models; and 5) relevant parameters and steps used to numerically evaluate the accuracy of the model, using the chi-square method.

To be included with the written report:

A. Printout of the MathCAD files used and created to:

Model the traffic signals

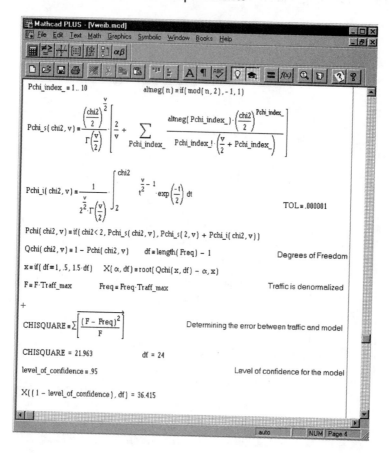

Figure 4 Chi-Square Method of Statistical Validation

Obtain optimum parameters of probabilistic models

Model validation using the chi-square method

B. Histogram of three traffic models analyzed

C. Sets of candidate models for each traffic data set

D. Parameters and plot of the pdf (probability distribution function) for each candidate model

E. Model histogram vs. traffic histogram and chi-square evaluation for a 95% level of confidence

4.15 Experimental Design in Computer Networks: A Case Study

by

J.C. Olabe and M.A. Olabe

Objective: This laboratory helps the student understand the computational requirements of simulation studies of complex communication networks and presents techniques of experimental design that will increase the efficiency of the simulation process while maintaining the validity of the study and the accuracy of the results.

Brief Description: A communications network connects six nodes via point-to-point links and a central routing node. The network traffic is defined by a highly nonsymmetric traffic matrix. A simulation study is to be implemented to evaluate the impact of upgrading the transmission rate of 10 communication links in the network's performance. A complete and exhaustive analysis of all new designs would require the simulation of over 1000 different networks ($2^{10} = 1024$). In this project, the students: 1) use techniques of experimental design to reduce the number of designs to a manageable number (16 different networks) while maintaining the validity of the study; 2) simulate, using COMNET III, this reduced set; and 3) evaluate the simulation results to determine the impact of each individual transmission link on the overall network performance.

Audience: Electrical engineering, telecommunications, and networking students at the junior or senior level, with a good background in probability and statistics, queuing theory, and the use of simulation in network analysis and performance evaluation.

Equipment: Excel is used to facilitate the implementation of a fractional-factorial experimental design. COMNET III is used to model and simulate the 16 alternative networks. Finally, Excel is again used to analyze the simulation results and evaluate the impact of each individual transmission link in the overall network performance.

Duration: Two laboratory sessions: 1) design of a fractional-factorial experimental design, and modeling and simulation of the 16 alternative networks; and 2) analysis of simulation results. Finally, one to two hours will be dedicated to documenting the project in a written report.

PROCEDURE:

1. **Initial model creation:** This laboratory focuses on the need for experimental design techniques and a methodical procedure to implement them. For this reason, the topology of the problem network is simple, and the traffic between nodes is highly nonsymmetric. The combined effect of these two properties minimizes the resolution of the required experimental designs. The problem network consists of six traffic-generating nodes and a central routing switch. Figure 1 shows the topology of the problem network. Initially, all communication links have a transmission rate of 1.5 Mbps. The goal of the experiment is to determine how many of 10 candidate links should be upgraded to 6 Mbps, and how each one of these changes will affect the overall network performance.

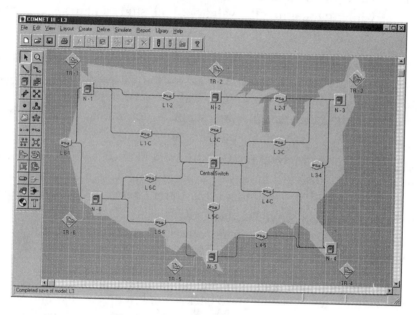

Figure I Network Topology

2. **Implementation of experimental design:** An exhaustive analysis of all possible alternatives to the problem would require the modeling and simulation of over 1000 different variations of the network ($2^{10} = 1024$). This search (factorial experimental design) not only has prohibitive dimensions and time requirements but also is highly inefficient: it searches for information that does not exist or is irrelevant, such as the interaction effect of two links on opposite sides of the network. A more desirable design targets those combinations of the total group of 1024 that would yield the desired information while dramatically reducing the computational power required. There is, of course, a trade-off between simulations reduction and the capacity of detecting the effects of link capacity changes in the overall network performance. It is the task of the students to determine the goals of the simulation before implementing the experimental design. Figure 2 shows an Excel file with the implementation of a 2^{10-7} design, where 16 combinations of the total 1024 are selected.

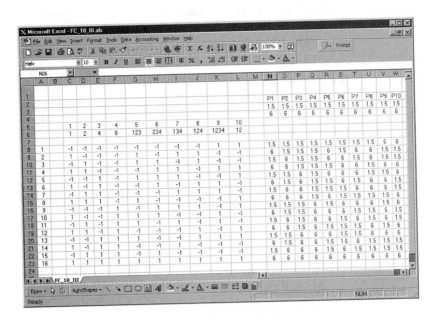

Figure 2 Excel Implementation of a 2^{10-7} Design

3. **Network modeling and experimental set:** After the experiment goals have been defined, and the experimental design implemented, the students create a total of 16 COMENT III files, in which one or several of the 10 eligible links are upgraded from 1.5 Mbps to 6 Mbps. A value of -1 in the experimental design implies no change in the 1.5-Mbps transmission rate of that particular link, while a value of +1 requires the upgrade to 6 Mbps.

4. **Simulation and data collection:** The simulation of the 16 selected networks is intended to collect data that will be used to evaluate the impact of each individual link change in the overall network performance or in some localized segments of it. For this reason, it is important to activate those report elements that will later be used for the evaluation. Although many parameters, or combinations of parameters, could be used to evaluate the performance of a network, for simplicity, packet delay is selected in this experiment as the goal of network optimization.

5. **Analysis of simulation results:** The experimental design selected for this laboratory, 2^{10-7} fractional factorial design, is characterized as having resolution 3 (III). The parameter resolution of an experiment is an indication of the type of information that can be drawn from the experiments. As was mentioned earlier, the greater the reduction (1024 to 16), the greater the loss of information. Resolution III indicates that all main effects of the link can be determined from the simulation data. In addition, a single two-way effect, if it existed, could be determined. The procedure to determine the main effects of each link is simple and directly obtained from the experimental design (Figure 2). Those changes associated with small effects would be rejected, and those link changes associated with sizable or large effects would be recommended.

6. **Conclusions and documentation:** The written report will describe: 1) the COMNET III original file used to model the problem network; 2) the definition of relevant information to be obtained from the simulation study; 3) the Excel file used to implement the fractional factorial design; 4) a critical evaluation of the 16 report files obtained during simulation; 5) a description of the method used to obtain the main effects of each transmission link from the simulation data, and the equations used to implement them; and 6) the recommendations to upgrade one or several links.

To be included with the written report:

A. Printout of the original COMNET III file

B. Printout of the Excel experimental design file

C. Summary of the data used in the 16 *.c3 COMNET III files

D. Summary of the 16 report files containing:

Simulation length

Packet delay statistics

Packets in transit statistics

Average link utilization

E. Numerical results of the simulation data analysis

F. List of equations used for data analysis

PART 5

WEB-BASED LABS

5.1 Constructing a Web-based Tutorial about High-Speed Modems

by

Ann Burroughs

Objective: The student will practice using search tools on the Internet to find and retrieve information about modems. The student will distill large amounts of fairly technical information and represent it in his/her own words. The student will develop HTML coding skills in the process of condensing and organizing the material for presentation. Students may eventually see the completed work of others doing this exercise, and can compare and contrast their own work.

Brief Description: Construct a Web-based tutorial about one of these topics: a) high-speed modems (56 kbps); b) ISDN modems; c) cable modems; or d) ASDL modems.

Audience: General, but computer and Web literate. A knowledge of HTML coding is helpful, but not necessary. There are many good sources for learning HTML online, and this assignment requires only minimal images and links.

Equipment: Any computer with a Web browser and an editor suitable for HTML coding. It is helpful if the student has a place to host home pages; otherwise the assignment will need to be submitted on disk.

Duration: Two weeks.

PROCEDURE:

The student will use search tools on the Internet to find and retrieve information about modems. Further, the student will develop HTML coding skills in the process of organizing the material for presentation.

Working as an individual or in teams of no more than two students, construct a Web-based tutorial about one of the following types of modems:

   a. high-speed modems (56 kbps)

   b. ISDN modems

   c. cable modems

   d. DSL (ADSL) modems.

Your tutorial should address these questions:

1. What is the purpose of a modem? (Briefly.)

2. Why do we need modems which can achieve better than 28.8 kbps?

3. How does the modem that you have chosen work? In particular, assuming a transfer rate of about 2400 baud over a dial-up phone line, how do high-speed modems attain transfer rates of up to 56 kbps? How do ISDN transfers at 64 kbps occur? How do cable modems achieve multiple megabits per second? How does (A)DSL achieve 1.5 Mbps?

    Probably the easiest topic on which to find information is high-speed modems. If you choose this topic, discuss trellis-coded modulation and modem constellation points, the number of signal events a high-speed modem uses and the number of bits encoded in each signal event. However, is it possible for 56 kbps data rates to be attained over dial-up lines?

4. Your tutorial should take advantage of the hypermedia medium. This means effective use of illustrations and links. There are many images already available on the Web.

5. You must have a bibliography page indicating where you got the information for your tutorial. Make sure you credit the source for any images you capture and use! (To capture an image, put the mouse in the image and depress the right mouse button; then follow instructions.)

6. You must turn in this lab by making it available on your Web page. The *lab1.html* page should be a title page which includes the name(s) of the students. Links to the substance of the tutorial should be available from this page. One way to do this is to include a table of contents in this title page. Another way is to write a brief summary of your tutorial with appropriate keyword links.

7. If you have never coded HTML, begin by following the tutorial available at *www.humboldt.edu/~help/webdev.web1*. Of course, you can also view the source for Web pages that appeal to you to see how particular effects are created.

8. Assume that your readers are generally familiar with computers and have used modems, but are trying to learn more and understand how modems work by reading your pages. You want to make your pages interesting and informative at the same time.

5.2 HTML Laboratory

by

Lawrence J. Osborne

Objective: To introduce students to the use of HTML, the World Wide Web and interactive network interfaces.

Brief Description: The students will include everything that a normal resume includes: education, experience, recreational activities and skills. In addition, this resume should have a scanned picture of the student, as well as an audio recording that gives his/her semester schedule.

Audience: Undergraduate students who are familiar with a computer.

Equipment: Access to the World Wide Web.

Duration: 10 days.

PROCEDURE:

Build an electronic resume which includes a scanned picture of yourself and an audio recording that gives your semester schedule. Include your name, address, phone and e-mail address, as well as your education, work experience, recreational activities and skills.

You are also to create a Homework Registration Form that will include data entry fields that allow a user to send information about him/herself. It should contain a button that, when pressed, reads the form and sends the contents of the text fields to the instructor's e-mail address. Finally, create a link from your resume to this form.

To turn in your homework, use the Registration Form. The URL field should contain the location of your resume. The URL will be used to read your resume and test your registration form.

PART 6
NETWORKING PCS

6.1 Converting a Stand-alone Windows-3.11 PC to a Networked PC

by

Samir and Ahlam Tannouri

Objective: To convert a stand-alone Windows-3.11 PC to a networked PC.

Brief Description: Students will convert a stand-alone PC to a networked one.

Audience: Students with knowledge of networking protocols and hardware.

Equipment:

♦ Crimper tool

♦ Category 5 patch cable

♦ One pair of RJ-45 wire connectors (per PC)

♦ An already existing installation of Windows 3.11

♦ A copy of the Windows setup file

♦ One network Card (per PC)

♦ One Hub (one available port for each PC to be networked).

Duration: Two hours.

PROCEDURE:

Convert a stand-alone Windows-3.11 PC to a Networked PC.

1. Make a patch cable.

2. Connect hub.

3. Install network card.

4. Check network card connection:

   a. Connect patch cable to the hub.

   b. Connect patch cable to the network card (NIC).

5. Upgrade Win 3.11 using TCP/IP information:

   a. Open into Network Group and open Network Setup.

   b. Set Network to Microsoft Networking without any other network.

   c. Add Network Card Adapter using DETECT option.

   d. Add TCP/IP protocol using Add Protocol (located on diskette).

   e. Highlight TCP/IP and make it the default protocol.

   f. Set up TCP/IP.

     1. Enter the IP address (e.g., 158.103.blding.pc).

     2. Enter the Gateway address (e.g., 15.103.1.100).

     3. Go to the DNS (Domain Name Servers) address
(e.g., 158.103.5.14 and 158.103.5.17).

     4. Enter the computer name (e.g., PC) and domain (morgan.edu).

     5. Go to the WINS configuration and mark the Enable box.

   g. Click on File and Printer Sharing:

     1. Click on File Sharing (if desired).

     2. Click on Printer Sharing (if desired).

   h. Click OK.

   i. Go to Control Panel and make sure to input:

   The workgroup name and name of PC.

6.2 Converting a Stand-alone Windows-95 PC to a Networked PC

by

Samir and Ahlam Tannouri

Objective: To convert a stand-alone Windows-95 PC to a networked PC.

Brief Description: Students will convert a stand-alone PC to a networked one.

Audience: Students with knowledge of networking protocols and hardware.

Equipment:

- ♦ Crimper tool
- ♦ Category 5 patch cable
- ♦ One pair of RJ-45 wire connectors (per PC)
- ♦ An already existing installation of Windows 95
- ♦ A copy of the Windows setup file
- ♦ One network card (per PC)
- ♦ One hub (one available port for each PC to be networked)

Duration: Two hours

PROCEDURE:

1. Make a patch cable.

2. Connect hub.

3. Install network card.

4. Check network card connection:

   a. Connect patch cable to the hub.

   b. Connect patch cable to the network card (NIC).

5. Install network drivers for Windows 95:

   a. Click on Start (located at the bottom window on the task bar).

   b. Click on Setting.

148

c. Click on Control Panel.

d. Click on Network.

e. Click on Add.

f. Choose Protocol on list.

g. Choose TCP under Microsoft.

h. Click OK (this will allow the computer to detect the network and will also install Client for Microsoft Networking).

i. Highlight TCP.

j. Click on Properties.

k. Set up TCP/IP:

1. Enter IP address (e.g., 158.103.blding.pc).

2. Enter the Gateway address (e.g., 15.103.1.100).

3. Go to the DNS (Domain Name Servers) address
   (e.g., 158.103.5.14 and 158.103.5.17).

4. Go to the WINS configuration and mark the Enable DNS box.

l. Click on Identification:

1. Enter the computer name (e.g., PC) and domain (e.g., morgan.edu).

m. Click on File and Printer Sharing:

1. Click on File Sharing (if desired).

2. Click on Printer Sharing (if desired).

n. Make sure that the CD-ROM with CAB file is in the D holder.

o. Click OK.

p. If the computer asks for CAB file, use Browse to indicate CD-ROM.

q. Reboot PC.

r. Check Network connection:

1. Click on Start.

2. Click on Programs.

3. Click on Windows Explorer.

4. Change directory to Neighborhood Network.

5. Look around to see other computers, and the job is done.

(*Note:* If you can't see other computers, review steps.)

6.3 Linking Two Computers

by

Samir and Ahlam Tannouri

Objective: To convert two stand-alone PCs into two interlinked PCs in a client/server model where the client uses the server's drives and printers.

Brief Description: Students will convert two stand-alone PCs to two interlinked PCs, so they can use one computer to access data and run programs on the other computer while also using the other's printer.

Audience: Students with a knowledge of networking protocols and hardware.

Equipment: Hardware needed:

- A free serial port on both computers, or a free parallel port on both computers.

- A 3-wire serial cable, 7-wire null-modem serial cable, or bidirectional parallel cable.

- 16 KB of free memory on the client computer and 130 KB of free memory on the server computer.

- Software needed: MS-DOS version 6.0 on one computer and MS-DOS version 6.0 or later on the other.

Duration: Two hours.

PROCEDURE:

There are many ways to establish a link between two computers:

- In this laboratory exercise, use the DOS programs INTERSVR and INTERLNK with the following steps:
  —Secure a physical connection: e.g., a null modem (cable).
  —Run Interlnk on the client computer and modify the CONFIG.SYS file.
  —Run the Intersrv on the server computer.

When two computers are connected using Interlnk, the server's drives appear as additional drives for the client and use additional names (i.e., F, G, H ...), so the client can use them as if they were its own drives.

Hint: You may use DOS help capability to assist you in doing the job. At the DOS prompt type: < help interlnk.exe >.

Method:

A. Physical connection:

1. Connect the two computers by the appropriate link using the chosen cable (i.e., a null-modem cable).

B. Setup the client computer:

1. Run INTERLNK.EXE on the client computer.

2. Update CONFIG.SYS file by changing the "device" entry to the new number of drives (total of client and server drives), e.g., device=c:\dos\interlnk.exe /drives:5

3. Save changes, and restart the computer (CTRL+ALT+DEL).

4. Type <interlnk> to see the new connection and learn about the redirected drives and ports.

C. Interlnk establishes connections between all redirected drives and ports when you do one of the following:

1. Restart the client computer when the server is running.

2. Type <interlnk> at the command prompt of the client computer.

3. Make one of the redirected drives on the client computer the active drive.

4. To break the connection, stop the server by pressing <ALT> + F4 on the server's keyboard.

5. To restart the server, type <intersrv> at the server's command prompt.

PART 7
NOVELL NETWARE LABS

7.1 Novell NetWare (3.12) Installation

by

Nizar Al-Holou and Mohannad Murad

Objective: To introduce the Novell network operating system, overview the hardware and software requirements of the system, install the hardware, install NetWare software, and setup the workstations.

Brief Description: Novell NetWare is a network operating system designed to connect two or more computers and other peripherals for the purpose of sharing data and equipment. A Novell local area network environment basically consists of a single central file server and a number of clients or workstations connected to it. The primary purpose of the file server is to allow client computers to store and share files. The file server can also provide various levels of security and access control, allowing a system manager to determine who has access to which resources.

Audience: Students with hardware and software experience.

Equipment:

Hardware: The hardware requirements to build a Novell (3.12) network are:

- A 386 or better PC for the file server with at least 6 MB RAM and 20 MB hard disk or more.

- A 286 or faster PC for the workstation.

- Network interface card (NIC) in every workstation and in the file server.

- Coaxial cable.

- T connectors.

- Two network terminators to indicate the end of the network.

Software:

- NetWare operating system at the file server.

- NetWare DOS requester on every workstation.

- DOS 3.3 or better.

- Driver software for the network cards in the file server and the workstations.

Duration: Three hours.

PROCEDURE:

I. HARDWARE INSTALLATION:

Before you start the process of the NetWare software installation, the relevant hardware should be installed and set up properly. To do so, observe the following steps:

A. Install Ethernet Cards:

Every computer in a local-area network (LAN) needs a network interface card (NIC) to provide the hardware interface between each workstation and the file server through a cabling system. NIC is an I/O device in a workstation that handles all transmission aspects, such as frame transmission, reception, and filtering. There are different types of network technologies. Ethernet is the most widely used LAN technology, which uses bus topology. The NIC used in this lab is an Ethernet card such as NE1000 and NE2000. Ethernet uses 48-bit Ethernet physical address cards.

1. Boot your computer with DOS to ensure that every PC is working properly.
2. Turn the computer off.
3. Remove the cover of the CPU of that computer.
4. Choose any empty expansion slot.
5. Insert your Ethernet card in that slot until it is completely seated.
6. Insert any screws that are needed to hold the card.
7. Replace the cover.
8. Repeat the same steps for all other computers.

B. Connecting the Ethernet Cards:

Ethernet is a bus topology and uses different wiring schemes depending on the type of cabling systems. You can use three different types of cables: Thick Ethernet Coaxial cable (Thicknet, 10Base-T), Thin Ethernet Coaxial cable (Thinnet, 10Base-2), and Twisted Pair (10Base-T). In this lab, you will use Thin Ethernet Coaxial cables. For each Ethernet card you need a T connector that connects the card to the Coaxial cable, as shown in the following figure. A 50-ohm terminator must also be inserted at each end of the main bus connecting your network to indicate the end of the network.

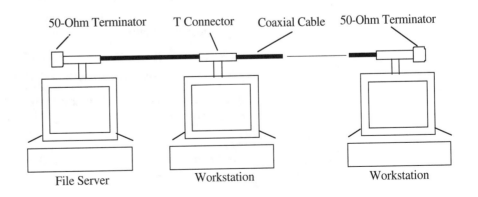

II. SOFTWARE INSTALLATION:

The installation process will destroy all the information on the hard disk of the file server. Therefore, before you start the process of file-server installation, make sure that all data on the hard disk of the PC operating as a file server has been copied onto a tape or Zip cartridge.

A. Create DOS partition:

1. Insert the DOS system diskette labeled "INSTALL" in drive A and boot the file server.

2. At the DOS prompt, type FDISK.

3. This command is used to create a bootable DOS partition on C drive so that the file server can boot from its hard drive. Select option (1) "Create DOS partition." Choose option (1), "Create DOS primary partition." This partition requires at least 8 MB. Go back to the first menu and choose option (3), "Select bootable partition." Choose the number that refers to the DOS primary partition that you have just created. Then exit FDISK by pressing <escape>.

4. Format the DOS partition by typing FORMAT C: /X/S.

5. Take the floppy disk out of drive A and reboot your machine to make sure that the partition you created is working properly.

B. Install File Server:

1. Insert the disk labeled "Install" in drive A and change the current drive to A by typing A:

2. Type INSTALL to start installing the file server.

3. From the screen menu, choose the option "Install new NetWare v3.12" and press < ENTER >.

4. Choose the option "Retain current disk partitions" and press < ENTER >.

5. You will be prompted to enter an optional file-server name. You may enter ECE_SRVR as the file-server name. Enter a name and press < ENTER >.

6. You will be prompted again to enter a number for your internal IPX. Enter a number and press < ENTER >. This number represents the number of the internal IPX and can be anywhere between 00 and FFFFFFFF.

7. At this point, you should get a message asking you to insert the diskette labeled "Netware 3.12 SYSTEM_1" in drive A. Insert the diskette and press < ENTER > to confirm the copying procedure.

8. You will be asked to insert the diskettes labeled SYSTEM_1, SYSTEM_2, and the diskette labeled UNICODE. Insert these diskettes labeled in order.

9. Enter the Country Code as 001 for United States, the Code Page as 437 for United States English, and the Keyboard Mapping as United States. Then press < F10 >.

10. When you are asked about the format you desire, choose the option "DOS Filename Format."

11. For the question "Do you want to specify any special startup set commands?" choose "No."

12. For the question "Do you want AUTOEXEC.BAT to load SERVER.EXE?" choose "No."

If you have completed all the previous steps successfully, the file SERVER.EXE should be loaded and run.

C. Install Drivers:

1. You need to load hard disk drives. Depending on the type of the hard drive in your computer, your command may change. For example, if you have an ISA disk, type LOAD A:ISADISK; then press < ENTER >.

2. After you have loaded the hard disk driver, run the file server installation program by typing LOAD C:\SERVER.312\INSTALL and then pressing <ENTER >.

3. Select "Disk Options" and "Partition Tables."

4. Select "Create Netware Partition" option; then press < ENTER >.

5. Confirm the partition information by pressing < ESC >, then choosing YES.

6. Press < ESC > twice to go back to the Installation Options.

7. Choose the "Volume Options."

8. Press < INSERT > to create a new volume. The new Volume Information window will appear on your screen.

9. Confirm the Volume Information by pressing < ESC >, then YES. As a result, the SYS volume will be created.

10. Press < Enter > to modify the SYS volume.

11. Use the arrow keys to go to the STATUS field and then press < ENTER >.

12. Choose the option "Mount Volume."

13. Press < ESC > twice to go back to the Installation Options.

14. Choose the option "System Options" and press < ENTER >.

15. Choose the option "Copy System and Public Files" and press < ENTER >.

16. Insert the diskettes in the proper order as the computer asks you to do so.

17. Now you are ready to create the STARTUP.NCF file. In order to create this file, you should select the option "Create STARTUP.NCF File" and then press < ENTER >.

18. Press < ENTER > again to accept the path.

19. In order to save STARTUP.NCF, press < ESC >, then YES.

20. Now it is time to load the LAN drivers. To do so, press < ALT+ESC >, which takes you back to the file-server prompt. Then type LOAD NE2000 (assuming the Ethernet card is NE2000).

21. Bind the LAN driver to the IPX protocol by typing: BIND IPX TO NE2000.

22. Enter a unique eight-digit hexadecimal number to be used as the Network number. After this, you should get a message saying, "IPX LAN protocol bound to Novel NE2000."

23. Press < ALT+ESC > to go back to the installation window.

24. Highlight the option "Create AUTOEXEC.NCF File" and press < ENTER >.

25. Save the AUTOEXEC.NCF by pressing <ESC>, then choosing YES.

The Installation process of the file server is now complete. Exit the installation utility by pressing < ESC > twice, then choosing YES.

WORKSTATION SETUP:

In order for a workstation to be properly set up and attached to the file-server, the following steps should be taken:

1. Boot the computer to make it one of the network workstations.

2. On the root, create a new directory with the name NET by typing MD NET and pressing <ENTER>.

3. Move into that subdirectory by typing CD NET and pressing <ENTER>.

4. Ask your instructor to give you the diskette that includes the workstation files. These files are LSL.COM, NE1000.EXE or NE2000.EXE, IPXODI.COM and NETX.EXE.

5. Make a copy of these files to the subdirectory NET created in step 2.

6. Go back to the root and open the AUTOEXEC.BAT file by typing EDIT AUTOEXEC.BAT and pressing <ENTER>.

7. Add the following lines to your AUTOEXEC.BAT file:

```
LSL
NE2000
IPXODI
NETX
```

We are assuming that you are using the Ethernet card NE2000. However, if you are using another Ethernet card, such as the NE1000 card, the second line should be NE1000.

8. Go back to the NET subdirectory.

9. Create a new file with the name NET.CFG by typing EDIT NET.CFG and pressing <ENTER>.

10. Inside NET.CFG, type the following code:

```
LINK DRIVER NE2000
INT 5
PORT 300
FRAME ETHERNET_802.3
```

If you are using another Ethernet card, then the first line should be changed accordingly.

11. Save your file and exit the EDIT program.

12. While the file sever is being loaded and run, reboot your workstation.

13. You should get a message saying that the workstation has been attached to the file server.

III. REFERENCES:

1. Ramos, E., Schroeder, A., and Beheler, A. (1996), *Networking Using Novell Netware (3.12)*, Prentice Hall, Englewood Cliffs, NJ.

2. Netware V3.11: System Manager, Novell Education.

3. Novell Netware V3.11, System Installation.

4. Corrigan, P. H., and Guy, A. (1989), *Building Local Area Networks with Novell Netware*, M&T Books.

7.2 Establishing User Accounts Using the SYSCON Utility Using Novell Netware (3.12)

by

Nizar Al-Holou and Mohannad Murad

Objective: To teach Novell system administration

Brief Description:

♦ Teach the student how to change the password of a user, create accounts for new users, manipulate account restrictions on a user account, put time restrictions on a user account, limit the disk space of a user account. Introduce the concept of Trustee Rights and show how to set Trustee Directory/File Assignments.

Audience: Students with a knowledge of computer systems and networks.

Equipment: SYSCON Utility, Novell NetWare 3.12.

Duration: Three hours.

PROCEDURE:

SYSCON is the most important utility provided by Novell and is used to create the basic setup for the network. With this utility, the supervisor can create user accounts, change a user password, delete a user account, create restrictions on a user account, create login scripts and manage many other important aspects, as shown below:

- Full Name
- Managed Users And Groups
- Managers
- Member List
- Other Information
- Trustee Directory Assignments

- Default Account Balance/Restrictions
- Default Time Restrictions
- Edit System AUTOEXEC File
- File Server Console Operators
- Intruder Detection/Lockout
- System Login Script
- View File Server Error Log

- Accounting
- Change Current Server
- File Server Information
- Group Information
- Supervisor Options
- User Information

- Account Restriction
- Change Password
- Full Name
- Groups Belonged To
- Login Script
- Managed Users And Groups
- Managers
- Other Information
- Security Equivalencies
- Station Restrictions
- Time Restrictions
- Trustee Directory Assignments
- Trustee File Assignments
- Volume/Disk Restrictions

SETTING THE SUPERVISOR'S PASSWORD:

1. In your workstation type F:, then press < ENTER >.

2. Log in by typing Login Supervisor and < ENTER >.

3. Change your current directory to Public directory by typing: CD \PUBLIC and < ENTER >.

4. Start the SYSCON utility by typing SYSCON, then press < ENTER>.

5. Choose the topic "User Information," then press < ENTER >.

6. Select SUPERVISOR, then press < ENTER >. The supervisor information box will appear on the right side of the screen.

7. Choose the option "Change Password," then press < ENTER >.

8. At this point you can enter the new password twice. The second time is for verification purposes.

   At this point, you may test the password that has just been created. Log out first and then login again using the new password, as in the following steps.

1. Press < ESC > three times, then choose YES.

2. At the F prompt, type Logout.

3. Log in again by typing Login Supervisor and then < ENTER >.

4. Enter the new password at the password prompt, then press < ENTER >. If the system logs you in, you have done the previous steps correctly.

Note that the supervisor account is very powerful and should not be used too frequently. Therefore, it is recommended that the supervisor create an additional account for him or herself and give this new account the ability to do most of the tasks he or she usually needs to do on a daily basis.

ESTABLISHING ACCOUNTS/PASSWORDS FOR NEW USERS:

Login account/password represents the first level of Network Security and controls the initial access to the network, as shown in the following login algorithm.

```
# Login Security Algorithm

  Access = False
  While Access = False Repeat
    Input User Name
      If Password needed then
      {
        Input Password
        If username match and Password match
          then Access = True
      }
    Else If Username match then Access = True
    End If
  End While
# Initial Access procedure
```

1. At your workstation, run the SYSCON utility, as you did before, by typing SYSCON and then pressing < ENTER >.

2. Highlight the topic "User Information" and press < ENTER > to see a list of the available users' names.

3. Press the < INSERT > key to add a new user name.

4. Enter any user name for the new user and press < ENTER >. A typical user name usually consists of a combination of the user's last name and initials.

5. Press < ESC > to reject the box with the title "Path to Create User's Home Directory." The new user name should appear on the list of user names.

6. While the new user name is highlighted, press < ENTER >. The User Information box should appear on the right side of the screen.

7. Move the cursor to the option "Change Password" and press <ENTER >. Type a temporary password in the Password Box.

The supervisor usually chooses temporary passwords for all new users. The user can change these passwords at any time and should do so periodically.

DEFINING ACCOUNT RESTRICTIONS:

1. From the first menu inside SYSCON, choose the topic "User Information."

2. Highlight the user name you have created and press < ENTER >.

3. From the "User Information" menu, choose the option "Account Restrictions" and press < ENTER >.

4. Move the cursor to the field "Limit Concurrent Connections." Press Y, then <ENTER > to limit the number of connections.

5. To restrict the ability of any user to log in to only one machine at a time, press 1 in the "Maximum Connections" field, then < ENTER >.

6. Move the cursor to the field "Allow User to Change Password." Press Y, then <ENTER >. Now the user can change his or her password whenever needed.

TIME RESTRICTIONS:

The following steps show you how to restrict the user's access time:

1. Log in as the supervisor and run the SYSCON utility.

2. From the first menu inside SYSCON, choose the topic "User Information."

3. Highlight the name of the user forwhom wish to create time restrictions on his or her account and press < ENTER >.

4. From the "User Information" menu choose the option "Time Restrictions" and press < ENTER >.

5. Move the cursor to the row of the current day (the day on which this experiment is run).

6. Insert spaces instead of the existing asterisks for the time the user is not allowed to log in. Each asterisk represents a half-hour interval. A space indicates that the user is not allowed to use his or her account during this time

interval. Therefore, by inserting spaces in the row of the current day for our user, you can prevent the user from using his or her account during this specific day.

TO CHECK YOUR WORK:

The supervisor should log out and log in as a new user to test the new user's setup as follows:

1. To exit the SYSCON utility, press < ESC > four times, then press < ENTER >.

2. Type Logout and press < ENTER >.

3. Try to log in as the new user during the allowed time by typing Login "User Name" and pressing < ENTER >, then typing the password of the new user.

4. Try to log in as the new user during the time which is not allowed by typing Login "User Name" and pressing < ENTER >, then typing the password of the new user. During this time, you should get a message saying "Attempting to login during an unauthorized time period. The supervisor has limited the times that you can login to this server." If you get this message, it means that you have done the previous steps correctly.

ALLOCATING DISK SPACE FOR USERS:

The following steps show you how to restrict the user's space in the shared drive:

1. Login as the supervisor and run the SYSCON utility.

2. From the first menu inside SYSCON, choose the option "User Information."

3. Highlight the name of the user whose disk space you wish to limit and press < ENTER >.

4. From the "User Information" menu, choose the option "Volume/Disk Restrictions" and press < ENTER >.

5. Press < ENTER > to select the volume SYS.

6. To limit user's space, press Y in front of the question "Limit volume space?"

7. Type the space limit number (e.g., 2048 KB) in the field "Volume Space Limit" and press < ENTER >.

TO CHECK YOUR WORK:

The supervisor should log out and log in as a new user to test the new user's setup as follows:

1. To exit the SYSCON utility, press < ESC > five times, then press <ENTER >.

2. Type Logout and press < ENTER >.

3. Log in as the user by typing Login "User Name" and pressing < ENTER >, then typing the password.

4. Type Dir and press < ENTER >.

You should see a line in the screen saying 2097152 bytes free. That is equal to 2 MB (e.g., $2 \times 1024 \times 1024$).

TRUSTEE RIGHTS:

Each user has different kinds of permissions to directories in the file server. These also differ in the level of control that a user has over a specific directory. For example, one user may be able to read files from a directory but not to create or modify files in that directory. Another user, however, may have the ability to create or modify files in that directory. These permissions to directories are called Trustee Rights.

There are different types of Trustee Rights as follows:

1. Supervisory (S): The user has all rights over this directory.

2. Read (R): The user can read files stored in this directory.

3. Write (W): The user can write to files stored in this directory.

4. Create (C): The user can create files in this directory.

5. Erase (E): The user can delete files from this directory.

6. Modify (M): The user can modify what kind of control all users could have to files in this directory.

7. File Scan (F): The user can scan the names of files listed in this directory.

8. Access Control (A): The user can grant trustee rights to other users over the files in this directory.

EXAMPLES:

1. If a user has the trustee rights [R F] to files in the directory SYS:\PUBLIC, it means that he/she has Read and File Scan rights over these files.

2. If a user has the trustee rights [RWCEMF] to files in the directory SYS:\MAIL, it means that he/she has Read, Write, Create, Erase, Modify and File Scan rights over these files.

TRUSTEE DIRECTORY/FILE ASSIGNMENTS:

The supervisor assigns different trustee rights to the users over the directories and files in the file server.

In the following steps, you will learn how to assign trustee rights to a certain user over the directory SYS:PUBLIC by setting the Trustee Directory Assignments.

1. Log in as the supervisor and run the SYSCON utility.

2. From the first menu inside SYSCON, choose the topic "User Information."

3. Highlight the name of the user to whom you wish to grant the trustee rights.

4. From the "User Information" menu, choose the option "Trustee Directory Assignments" and press < ENTER >.

5. Press < INSERT > twice.

6. Press < ENTER > to choose the server with which you are working.

7. Press < ENTER > again to view the directories under the volume SYS.

8. Move the cursor to the directory PUBLIC and press <ENTER>. The name of the directory SYS:\PUBLIC should appear in the box titled "Directory In Which Trustee Should Be Added."

9. Press < ESC >, then < ENTER >. The directory SYS:\PUBLIC should be added in the box titled "Trustee Directory Assignments" with the rights [R F].

10. To add more rights, press < ENTER >, then < INSERT >.

11. To choose a new right to be added, move the cursor to that specific right and press <F5 >. For example, move the cursor to Write and press < F5 >, then move it to Create and press < F5 >.

12. Press < ENTER > to accept your selection. The new rights Write and Create should be added to the list "Trustee Rights Granted."

13. Press < ESC > to return to the "Trustee Directory Assignments."

14. Press < ESC > again to return to the "User Information" menu.

The process of assigning trustee rights to certain users over a specific file in the file server is accomplished by setting the "Trustee File Assignments" in a similar way to what we did before. This task is left to students as an exercise.

EXERCISES:

1. Use the SYSCON utility to create a new account for yourself.

2. Limit your concurrent connections to only one.

3. Restrict your login time to weekdays (Monday to Friday) from 8 a.m. to 5 p.m.

4. Give your account a free space of only 5 MB on the hard disk.

5. Give your account only the Read trustee over the subdirectory SYS:\SYSTEM.

REFERENCES

1. Ramos, E., Schroeder, A., and Beheler, A., (1996), *Networking Using Novell Netware (3.12)*, Prentice Hall, Englewood Cliffs, NJ.

2. *Netware V3.11*: System Manager, Novell Education.

3. *Novell Netware V3.11*, System Installation.

4. Corrigan, P. H., and Guy, A. (1989), *Building Local Area Networks with Novell Netware*, M&T Books.

7.3 Login Scripts Using Novell NetWare (3.12)

by

Nizar Al-Holou and Mohannad Murad

Objective: To introducing the concept of Login Scripts, study some of the important Login Script commands and their uses, and learn how to create a Login Script.

Brief Description: A Login Script is a set of commands written by the supervisor to set up the users' environment and executed every time a user logs in. There are three types of Login Scripts: System, User and Default. The System Login Script is executed first, and the User Login Script is executed afterward if it is available. SYSCON provides the Supervisor with a simple editor for creating and modifying both the System and the User Login Scripts.

Audience: Students with a knowledge of programming and networking.

Equipment: NetWare 3.12.

Duration: Three hours.

PROCEDURE:

A Login Script is a set of instructions written by the supervisor or user and executed during the login process. The **SYSCON** utility provides a simple editor for creating and modifying Login Scripts.

There are three types of Login Scripts:

1. System Login Script

2. User Login Script

3. Default Login Script

These types are executed as follows:

```
# Login Script Algorithm

  IF System Script is Available then
    {
      # System Script procedure
      ...
      ...
```

```
    }

End IF


IF User Script is Available then
    {
      # User Script procedure
      ...
      ...
      ...
    }
  End IF

  # Default Script procedure
  ...
  ...
...
```

The main purpose of having a Login Script is to set up the network and users' environment. This includes mapping a specific directory to appear as the root directory, displaying a message to the user, or sending a command to DOS. Since the supervisor can set a System Login Script using the "Supervisor Options Menu" inside the SYSCON utility, it is not possible to have a Login Script for each individual user. However, it is usually recommended that each user be given a Login Script to develop his or her own needs.

The following is an overview of some important Login Script commands and their uses.

ATTACH:

This command can be used in a Login Script to attach the user on a file server to a different file server on the same network.

For example, suppose we have three file servers—FileS_1, FileS_2 and FileS_3—connected to the same network. Also suppose that a user has the same user name and password for all file servers. This user could access any one of his/her accounts and could have a different Login Script for each account in each file server. If this user wants to be attached directly to FileS_2 after he/she logs in FileS_1, then the ATTACH command should be placed in his/her Login Script on FileS_1 as follows:

```
ATTACH FileS_2
```

Similarly, if this user wants to be connected to FileS_1 after he/she logs in FileS_2, the command ATTACH FileS_1 should be placed in his/her Login Script on FileS_2.

If this user has different user names and passwords on each file server, then he/she needs to indicate his/her user name and password in the ATTACH command as follows:

```
ATTACH FileS_1 / Myusername ; mypassword
```

Myusername and mypassword are the user's username and password on FileS_1, respectively.

BREAK:

If you have BREAK ON in the Login Script, you can halt the script's execution by holding down the CONTROL key and pressing BREAK. However, if you have BREAK OFF in the Login Script, the execution of the script cannot be stopped.

DRIVE:

The default drive of a Network is normally the first drive (usually drive F). By using the command DRIVE, the drive of a network can be set to any valid local or network drive letter, or to a number indicating the order in which the drive was mapped. For example, the command DRIVE *1: would set the default drive to the first network drive letter, which might be F.

The command DRIVE C: would set the default drive to be the local hard disk drive C.

DISPLAY:

This command is used to display a message contained in a file on the screen each time a user logs in. For example:

```
DISPLAY F:\PUBLIC\NOTICE.TXT
```

will display the contents of the file NOTICE.TXT on the screen each time a user logs in.

If the file contains non-ASCII control characters placed by a word processing program, then you need to use the FDISPLAY command instead of the DISPLAY command. FDISPLAY will filter out these control characters before printing the message on the screen.

DOS SET:

This command is used to set any DOS environment variable to any value. Note that it is also possible to type only the word SET instead of DOS SET.

Some examples are:

```
DOS SET USER = "MURAD"
SET PROMPT = "$P$B$T$G"
```

EXIT:

This command is used to terminate the execution of the Login Script and to start any DOS command, if needed. For example, if you want a directory listing each time you log in, include the following line at the end of your Login Script:

```
EXIT "DIR"
```

However, if you want to temporarily suspend the execution of the Login Script, run another DOS command or .EXE file, and resume with the Login Script after the DOS command is finished, use the symbol "#." For example, the command # DIR, if included in the middle of a Login Script, will give you a directory listing and return the control to the Login Script after that command is finished.

FIRE PHASERS

This command is used to generate an alarm sound to catch the user's attention. For example, the command:

```
FIRE PHASERS 4 TIMES
```

will cause the alarm to go off four times.

IF STATEMENT:

This command is used to test some conditions and execute certain commands based on the conditions tested. There are different structures of the IF statement, as you will see under the examples section. The operators used in the IF statement can be written as symbols or words as follows:

- To present an *equal to* operator, type IS, =, ==, or EQUALS.

- To present a *not equal to* operator, type IS NOT, !=, <>, #, DOES NOT EQUAL or NOT EQUAL TO.

- To present a *greater than* operator, type IS GREATER THAN or > .

- To present a *less than* operator, type IS LESS THAN or <.

- To present a *greater than or equal to* operator, type IS GREATER THAN OR EQUAL TO or >=.

- To present a *less than or equal to* operator, type IS LESS THAN OR EQUAL TO or <=.

To test the existence of two or more conditions at the same time, use the AND or "," operator. However, to test the existence of at least one condition among two or more conditions, use the OR operator.

There is a list of Login Script Variables that are set before the execution of the Login Script and can be used in your IF statement. Some of these variables and their possible values are shown below:

- The variable DAY could have any integer value between 01 and 31.

- The variable DAY_OF_WEEK could have any value between Sunday and Saturday.

- The variable MONTH could have any value between 01 and 12.

- The variable MONTH_NAM could have any value between January and December.

Note: All variables should be written in capital letters.

Examples

The following are IF statements to help students understand the syntax and use of an IF statement:

```
IF NEW_MAIL EQUALS YES THEN WRITE " *** New Mail ***"

IF DAY > "20" AND DAY_OF_WEEK != "Sunday" THEN BEGIN
FIRE PHASERS 4 TIMES
WRITE "Remember to pay the bills!"
END

WRITE:
```

This command is similar to the ECHO command in DOS. It displays the message following it on the screen at the same time it is executed.

Example: WRITE "Please Logout before leaving this machine"

In the message following the WRITE command, it is possible to use the same Login Script Variables discussed in the IF statement command. However, in order for the system to understand that you need to type the value of the variable DAY_OF_WEEK, not just the statement "DAY_OF_WEEK," you must precede that variable (or any other variable) with a "%."

For example, suppose the current day is Monday. Then, after the execution of the command:

```
WRITE "Today is %DAY_OF_WEEK"
```

the screen will display the message: Today is Monday. Another way to accomplish this is by typing the following line:

```
WRITE "Today is";DAY_OF_WEEK
```

Note that in order to display the message, you must use the symbol \. Also, in order to display a new line, you must use the symbol \n.

Example: WRITE "Today is:\n";DAY_OF_WEEK

If the current day is Monday, the output of the above command will be:

```
Today is
Monday
```

There are also four special symbols that can be used within the message following the WRITE command:

PAUSE:

This command halts the execution of the Login Script and displays the message "Strike a key when ready ...." The Login Script is resumed after pressing any key on the keyboard.

REMARK:

> This command is used before writing any comments needed only to understand the Login Script; it is skipped at the time of execution. Other alternatives are:
>
> ```
> REM, * or ; .
> ```

WRITING A LOGIN SCRIPT AND TESTING IT:

1. In your workstation type F: and <ENTER>.

2. Log in by typing Login Supervisor and <ENTER>.

3. Start the SYSCON utility by typing SYSCON and <ENTER>.

4. Choose the topic "User Information" and <ENTER>.

5. Highlight one of the users for whom you wish to create a Login Script.

6. Highlight the option "Login Scripts" from the User Information Menu and press <ENTER>.

7. A box saying that "Login Script does not exist" will appear. This box also allows you to make a copy from another user's Login Script by typing that user's name in front of the line "Read Script From User:"

8. Press <ENTER> to proceed.

9. A blank screen should appear and any Login Script can be typed in.

10. Type MAP S1:=SYS:\PUBLIC and <ENTER>.

11. Type MAP S2:=SYS:\LOGIN and <ENTER>.

12. Type WRITE "Today is %DAY_OF_WEEK" and <ENTER>.

13. Type

    ```
        IF DAY > "20" AND DAY_OF_WEEK != "Sunday" THEN BE-
    GIN
        FIRE PHASERS 4 TIMES
        WRITE "Remember to pay the bills!"
    END
    ```

14. Type FIRE PHASERS 3 TIMES.

15. Press <Esc> then <ENTER> to save what you typed before.

16. Press <Esc> three times, then <ENTER> to exit the SYSCON program.

17. Try to log in as the user for whom you created the previous Login Script and see the results of the previous Login Script.

Exercise:

Use the SYSCON utility to create a Login Script to the account you created for yourself in the previous lab. The Login Script should accomplish the following:

1. Map subdirectory SYS:\SYSTEM to be drive S1.

2. Map subdirectory SYS:\PUBLIC to be drive S2.

3. Start the alarm four times when the login day is your birthday, and type the message "Happy Birthday."

4. Remind you to give the rent to your landlord at the beginning of each month, except on Sundays.

REFERENCES:

1. Ramos, E., Schroeder, A., and Beheler, A., (1996) *Networking Using Novell Netware (3.12)*, Prentice Hall, Englewood Cliffs, NJ.

2. *Netware V3.11*: System Manager, Novell Education.

3. *Novell Netware V3.11*, System Installation.

4. Corrigan, P. H., and Guy, A. (1989), *Building Local Area Networks with Novell Netware*, M&T Books.

7.4 Network Security, Organization and Control Using Novell Netware (3.12)

by

Nizar Al-Holou and Mohannad Murad

Objective: To introduce Novell network security, organization and control, study the four levels of security in Novel Netware, study the organization of the network and the **GROUP** feature, and study the control of the network as a whole using **FCONSOLE**.

Brief Description: Novell provides four levels of security for users and system administrators. System administrators use this structure to organize the network. These four levels of security are:

1. Login passwords

2. Trustee rights

3. Directory rights

4. Directory rights

Audience: Students with hardware and software experience.

Duration: Three hours.

PROCEDURE:

INTRODUCTION:

One of the most important tasks of a supervisor is to create and organize a network structure in which some data can be shared by all users while simultaneously giving each user access to his or her own private data. In reality, the process of organizing the network structure and granting the users different rights to access files and directories is far more complicated than you might think. Some users have the right to edit or modify the contents of some directories while others do not. Likewise, a group of users might have some common tasks that make it easier for the supervisor to define them as a group and give them identical rights over some files or directories. The concept of granting the users some rights to access data while restricting other users is known as Network Security.

In addition to assigning different rights to different users, the supervisor must maintain control over the network. Using both the FCONSOLE.EXE program and the MONITOR utility, he/she can do this.

PASSWORDS:

Once a supervisor establishes a new account he/she might assign an arbitrary password to it. The user of that account can then change the password using the SET-PASS command. A password is a string of characters that must be entered by the user whenever he/she wants to log into the network. The supervisor can also determine the minimum length of a password and force the users to change their passwords periodically for security reasons.

Changing a password:

1. Type F: then press <ENTER>.

2. Log in as one of the users created in the previous labs, then enter the password of that user.

3. Type SETPASS and press <ENTER>. This command lets you change the old password into a new one.

4. The system will ask you to enter the old password for that user. Enter the old password and press <ENTER>.

5. The system will then ask you to enter the new password. Enter the new password and press <ENTER>.

6. The system will ask you to reenter the new password for verification reasons. Enter the new password again and press <ENTER>.

7. If your change was successful, a message saying that your password has been changed should appear on your screen. Otherwise, a message saying that your password has not changed will appear.

8. Log out by typing LOGOUT and <ENTER>.

9. To verify that you have you have changed your password, log in again and see if the system is accepting your new password.

Controlling the minimum length of a password and forcing the users to change their passwords periodically:

1. Type F: then <ENTER>.

2. Log in as the supervisor by typing Login Supervisor, then <ENTER>.

3. Enter password, then press <ENTER>.

4. Start the SYSCON utility by typing SYSCON, then <ENTER>.

5. Select the option User Information, then press <ENTER>.

6. Select the name of the user whose password you wish to control; then press <ENTER>.

7. From the User Information menu, select the option Account Restrictions; then press <ENTER>.

8. A box with the title "Account Restrictions For User …" should appear on your screen.

9. Select the option Require Password and type in Y to change it to "Yes"; then press <ENTER>.

10. Select the option Minimum Password Length. For example, type "10," then press <ENTER>. Here we have 10 digits as the minimum password length.

11. Select the option Force Periodic Password Changes and type Y to change it to "Yes"; then press <ENTER>.

12. Select the date on the "Date Password Expires" line.

13. Use the current date (in the lower right corner of your screen) as the expiration date.

14. Press <Esc> four times, then press <ENTER> to exit the SYSCON Utility.

15. Log out by typing Logout, then press <ENTER>.

16. Login again as the user whose account you restricted.

17. A message saying that the password has expired should appear on the screen and the system will ask you if you would like to change your password.

18. Press Y, then <ENTER>.

19. Type your new password. Since we have limited the minimum length of the password to 10 characters, the system will not accept your new password if it is less than 10 characters, and a message saying that the new password is too short should appear on your screen. Also, the system may not allow you to use a previously used password.

20. Type your new password again for verification.

TRUSTEE RIGHTS:

NetWare allows the supervisor to provide users with eight levels of rights (A, C, E, F, M, R, S, W). Trustee rights are the access rights assigned by the supervisor to users over some directories and files in the network. When rights are granted to users to access a directory, they have the right to access all of its subdirectories unless otherwise specified. The following is a list of the trustee rights and their meanings when they are granted for files and/or directories:

1. ACCESS CONTROL (A)

   For a directory, *access control* allows the user to grant his/her rights over that directory to other users.

   For a file, it allows the user to grant his/her rights over that file to other users.

2. CREATE (C)

   For a directory, *create* allows the user to create new files or directories under that directory. However, to write into a newly created file, you should have *write* privileges.

   For a file, it allows the user to recover or undelete a file that has been erased.

3.   ERASE (E): Allows the user to delete files or subdirectories under that directory.

4.   FILE SCAN (F): Allows the user to view the names of files and subdirectories.

5.   MODIFY (M): Allows the user to change the attributes or names of files and subdirectories under that directory

6.   READ (R): Allows the user to read files in that directory or file.

7.   SUPERVISORY (S): Gives the user all the rights over that directory/file (e.g., supervisory).

8.   WRITE (W): Allows the user to edit the contents of files or subdirectories.

The assignments of different trustee rights to different users over directories in the file server have been discussed in the Syscon Utility Lab, under the section "TRUSTEE DIRECTORY/FILE ASSIGNMENTS."

CONTROLLING DIRECTORY INHERITED RIGHTS:

When rights are granted to a user to access a directory, he/she inherits the rights to access all its subdirectories by default, unless otherwise specified. The supervisor can exclude some of the trustee rights to future subdirectories created under that original directory by specifying that in the inherited rights mask, using the FILER utility. For example, different users would have different rights to the directory SYSTEM, depending on what rights the supervisor assigned to them for that directory. For example, if the supervisor created a subdirectory with the name TOOLS under the SYSTEM directory, each user would normally inherit exactly the same rights for the new subdirectory as he/she would have for the original directory SYSTEM. However, the supervisor can mask the Erase right over the subdirectory TOOLS. This can be accomplished using the FILER utility as follows:

1.   Login as the supervisor.

2.   In the root directory, create a new subdirectory with the name TOOLS by typing MD TOOLS, then pressing <ENTER>.

3.   Move into the TOOLS subdirectory by typing CD TOOLS, then pressing <ENTER>.

4.   Type FILER, then press <ENTER>.

5.   Select the option Current Directory Information, then press <ENTER>.

6.   Choose the Inherited Rights Mask field, then press <ENTER>.

7.   Choose the option Erase Directory/File, then press <DELETE>.

8.   Press Y to confirm that.

9.   Press <Esc> until you exit the FILER utility.

10.   Log out by typing LOGOUT.

Now, any users other than supervisor-equivalent users are not allowed to inherit the MODIFY right, unless that right is specified directly in their trustee assignments list for that specific subdirectory.

At this stage you can check your work by checking the rights you have over the tools directory using the RIGHTS command. Move into the TOOLS directory and execute the command RIGHTS. This command will show you the effective rights you have over the TOOLS directory. The effective rights are the combination of those rights granted with the user trustee assignments, and the rights inherited from the parent directory after applying the inherited rights mask. It should show that you do not have the erase right over TOOLS directory.

FILE ATTRIBUTES:

File attributes is another level of security that NetWare provides. File attributes are similar to DOS file attributes which permit you to define the attributes of any file, such as sharable, read only, and so on. The most important attributes that a file can have are:

1. READ ONLY: Allows files to be read or executed, but does not allow users to modify or delete any file.

2. SHAREABLE: Allows files to be accessed by multiple users at the same time as long as they have appropriate rights.

3. HIDDEN: File will not appear in the directory.

4. SYSTEM: Sets the DOS SYSTEM attribute, which cannot be deleted or modified by the user.

5. TRANSACTIONAL: Changes to the file are either completed or ignored.

6. PURGE: The file cannot be recovered after it has been deleted.

7. EXECUTE ONLY: The file can only be executed and therefore should have the .EXE or .COM extension.

8. RENAME INHIBIT: The user cannot rename a file with this attribute.

9. DELETE INHIBIT: The user cannot delete a file with this attribute.

File attributes can be set by using either the FILER utility, as discussed previously, or the FLAG command in DOS, as shown below:

1. Log in as any of the users created in the previous labs.

2. Move to the root by typing CD\, then pressing <ENTER>.

3. Create a new subdirectory with the name lab4 by typing MD lab4, then <ENTER>.

4. Move into that subdirectory by typing CD lab4, then <ENTER>.

5. Type EDIT EX4.TXT <ENTER>. This step should create a new file with the name EX4.TXT and open that file for editing using the EDIT word processor.

6. Type any message inside EX4.TXT, then press <Alt> + F. Press S to save your work, then X to exit.

7. Once you are in DOS again, type FLAG EX4.TXT H, then press <ENTER>. By doing so, you are setting the file EX4.TXT to be HIDDEN.

8. Try to see if you have the file EX4.TXT in the lab4 subdirectory by typing dir, then pressing <ENTER>.

9. You should not find the file EX4.TXT under the lab4 directory.

10. Log out by typing LOGOUT, then <ENTER>.

GROUPS:

Each user in the network has his/her own account and access rights over files and directories in the network. However, the supervisor might prefer to classify the users under different groups—for example, Faculty and Students. Novell allows the supervisor to create groups of users that can be given the same rights. This feature makes it easier for the supervisor to organize the structure of his/her network. Moreover, the Group feature simplifies the job of granting access rights to users who can be gathered under one group. The supervisor could grant rights to the group as a whole only once rather than repeating the same work for each user under that group.

1. Login as the supervisor.

2. Start the SYSCON utility by typing SYSCON, then press <ENTER>.

3. Select the option "Group Information," then press <ENTER>.

4. Press <Insert> to add a New Group. A small box should appear asking for a New Group Name.

5. Type STUDENTS, then <ENTER>. This name should now appear under the Group Names list.

6. Select the group STUDENTS, then press <ENTER>. This should cause the Group Information menu to appear in the screen.

7. Select the option Member List, then press <ENTER>.

8. Press <Insert>. A list of Not Group Members should appear on your screen.

9. Select any user to be a member of the group Students and press <ENTER>. This user name should now appear under the Group Member list.

10. To add other users to the group STUDENTS, repeat steps 8 and 9.

11. Once you are finished adding users to your Group Members list, press <Esc> to return to the Group Information menu.

12. Select the option Trustee Directory Assignments, then press <ENTER>.

13. Press <Insert>. If you know the name of the Directory In Which Trustee Should Be Added, type in that name; otherwise, press <Insert> again.

14. While the name of your file server is selected, press <ENTER>.

15. While the volume SYS is selected, press <ENTER> again. A list of Network Directories should appear on your screen.

16. Assign trustee rights for the group STUDENTS over any directory. (See Syscon Lab under TRUSTEE DIRECTORY/FILE ASSIGNMENTS.)

FCONSOLE:

FCONSOLE (File Server Console) is a program that allows you to control console functions and access information that can be used to observe, analyze, and fine-tune the network activities. With FCONSOLE users can be monitored, warned of problems, or disconnected when they cause trouble. The following steps demonstrate some FCONSOLE uses.

1. Log in as the supervisor.

2. Using the SYSCON utility, create a new account and give it the username Guest.

3. Grant the account you just created to one of your friends and let him/her log into another machine using the username Guest.

4. Exit the SYSCON utility and go back to DOS.

5. Move into PUBLIC subdirectory by typing CD \PUBLIC, then <ENTER>.

6. Start the FCONSOLE program by typing FCONSOLE, then <ENTER>.

7. Select the option Connection Information, then press <ENTER>.

8. While your friend is still logging into the other machine, start typing the username Guest. The selected bar should move to the username Guest. Press <ENTER> while the name guest is selected.

9. Choose the option Broadcast Console Message, then press <ENTER>.

10. Type the message "Hello my friend" into the box, <ENTER>. This message should appear across the bottom of the screen belonging to the workstation where your friend guest is logged in.

11. Press <Ctrl> + <ENTER> to remove that message.

12. Select the option Other Information, then press <ENTER>.

13. Write down the number labeled Network Address. The eight digits on the left of the ":" represent the number of the network entered at the time of installation. However, the 12 digits on the right of ":" represent the number of the Network Card for the workstation used by the user TEST.

14. Press <Esc> four times, then press <ENTER> to exit the FCONSOLE utility.

15. Start the SYSCON utility by typing SYSCON, then pressing <ENTER>.

16. Select the option User Information, then press <ENTER>.

17. Select the username Guest, then press <ENTER>.

18. Select the option Station Restrictions, then press <ENTER>.

19. Press <Insert>.

20. In the box labeled Network Address, type the Network number consisting of the eight digits on the right of the ":" of the number you wrote down in step 13. This will restrict the access of user Guest for this network alone.

21. A question should appear in the screen asking you to "Allow the user to log in from any node." Press N for No, then press <ENTER> to add more restrictions.

22. In the Node Address box, type the network card of the workstation where the user Guest is logged in. This number consists of the 12 digits to the left of the ":" of the number you wrote down in step 13.

23. Press <Esc> four times, then press <ENTER> to exit the SYSCON utility.

By following the previous steps, the supervisor has restricted the access of the user Guest to the machine on which he was working.

Ask your friend with the username Guest to log out and let him/her try to log in with the same username Guest from any other workstation. Note what happens. Present the results to your instructor.

Exercises:

1. Run FCONSOLE again and explore its other options: Change Current File Server, Broadcast Console Message, Down File Server, and Version Information. Present the results to your instructor.

2. Restrict the access of the account you created in the Syscon Lab to only one specific workstation.

III. REFERENCES

1. Ramos, E., Schroeder, A., and Beheler, A., (1996), *Networking Using Novell Netware (3.12)*, Prentice Hall, Englewood Cliffs, NJ.

2. *Netware V3.11*: System Manager, Novell Education.

3. *Novell Netware V3.11*, System Installation.

4. Corrigan, P. H., and Guy, A. (1989), *Building Local Area Networks with Novell Netware*, M&T Books.

CONTRIBUTING FACULTY AUTHORS

NIZAR AL-HOLOU
Department of Electrical and Computer Engineering
University of Detroit Mercy
4001 W. McNichols Road
Detroit, MI 48219
alholoun@udmercy.edu

SHAKIL AKHTAR
Department of Computer Science
Central Michigan University
Mt. Pleasant, MI 48859
akhtar@cps.cmich.edu

ESSAID BOUKTACHE
Electrical Engineering Technology
Purdue University Calumet
bouktae@calumet.purdue.edu

ANN BURROUGHS
Computing Science Department
Humboldt State University
Arcata, CA 95521-8299
burroughsa@axe.humboldt.edu

KAMYAR DEZHGOSHA
Math/Computer Science Department
Central State University
Wilberforce, OH 45384
E-mail: Kamyar@cesvxa.ces.edu

BRUCE ELENBOGEN
CIS Department
University of Michigan-Dearborn
Dearborn, MI 48128
boss@umich.edu

FRANCES GRODZINSKY
Department of Computer Science and Information Technology
Sacred Heart University
5151 Park Avenue
Fairfield, CT 06432
grodzinskyf@sacredheart.edu

HERMAN HUGHES
Computer Science Department
Michigan State University
East Lansing, MI
hughes@cps.msu.edu

TED MIMS
Computer Science Department
University of Illinois at Springfield
Springfield, IL 62794
mims.ted@uis.edu

JUAN CARLOS OLABE
Electrical Engineering Department
Christian Brothers University
Memphis, TN 38104
jolabe@cbu.edu

MIGUEL ANGEL OLABE
Departamento de Electrónica y Telecomunicaciones
Escuela Tecnica Superior de Ingenieros Industriales y de Ingenieros de
        Telecomunicación de Bilbao (ETSII-IT)
Euskal Herriko Unibertsitatea (EHU)
C/ Alameda de Urquijo s/n
48013 Bilbao, Spain
jtpolbam@bicc00.bi.ehu.es

LAWRENCE J. OSBORNE
P.O Box 10056
Lamar University
Beaumont, TX 77710
osborne@hal.lamar.edu

PETER SANDERSON
Computer Science Department
Southwest Missouri State University
901 S. National Ave.
Springfield, MO 65804
dps910f@mail .smsu.edu

DAISY F. SANG
California State Polytechnic University
3801 West Temple Avenue
Pomona, CA 91768
fcsang@csupomona.edu

AHLAM TANNOURI
Computer Science Department
Morgan State University
Baltimore, MD 21251
atannour@Morgan.edu

SAMIR TANNOURI
Computer Science Department
Morgan State University
Baltimore, MD 21251
stannour@Morgan.edu

WILLIAM TETER
Computer Science Department
SUNY Plattsburgh
Plattsburgh, NY 12901
teterwa@splava.cc.plattsburgh.edu